TOTAL 4x4

THE DEFINITIVE GUIDE TO
4x4 SPORTS-UTILITY VEHICLES

ANDREW CHARMAN

p

This is a Parragon Book

First published in 2006

Parragon
Queen Street House
4 Queen Street
Bath BA1 1HE, UK

A copy of the CIP data for this book is available from the British Library upon request.

The rights of Andrew Charman to be identified as the author of this work have been asserted in accordance with Section 77 of the Copyright, Designs and Patents Act of 1988.

Created, designed, produced and packaged by Stonecastle Graphics Ltd

Designed by Paul Turner and Sue Pressley
Edited by Philip de Ste. Croix

Printed and bound in China

The author and publishers have made every reasonable effort to contact all copyright holders. Any errors that may have occurred are inadvertent and anyone who for any reason has not been contacted is invited to write to the publishers so that a full acknowledgement may be made in subsequent editions of this work.

ISBN: 1-40547-340-1

Photographic credits (a = above, b = below, c = centre, l = left, r = right):

© LAT Photographic Digital Archive: 5, 6, 10, 11, 12, 13, 14(al), 20(a), 24, 25(a), 26, 29, 30(b), 32(a), 33, 36(b), 37, 38, 39, 42, 43(a), 43(bl), 44, 47(a), 48, 49(a), 49(cr), 53, 54, 56, 57, 58, 59, 62, 64, 65, 70(a), 72, 73, 79(br), 82(a), 82(br), 86(a).

Giles Chapman Library: 7(a), 9(a), 16(a), 18, 20(b), 21, 25(b), 27, 28, 30(a), 31, 32(b), 34, 35, 36(a), 40, 41, 45, 46, 50, 51, 52(a), 55, 60, 61, 83(cr), 83(b).

Andrew Charman, plus the press offices of various featured motor manufacturers, for which special thanks: 1, 7(b), 8, 9(b), 14-15(b), 15, 16(b), 17, 19, 22, 23, 43(br), 47(b), 49(b), 52(b), 63, 66, 67, 68, 69, 70(b), 71, 74, 75, 76, 77, 78, 79(a), 79(bl), 80, 81, 82(bl), 83(ar), 84, 85, 86(b), 87, 88, 89, 90, 91, 92, 93, 94, 95.

Page 1: Today a host of SUVs are targeted at the most luxurious end of the market, with plush interiors and lots of equipment. Lincoln's Navigator is a typical example.

Contents

1 From Genesis to Recreation

The Sports-Utility Vehicle is a global phenomenon, and one which is just about the only sector of the motoring market still recording constant and indeed accelerating growth. Each year motor shows bulge with ever-growing numbers of brand-new SUVs, and the evidence suggests that hidden away in the tight secrecy of manufacturers' design studios, yet more are being created.

The SUV has become one of today's most popular classes of vehicle, despite early safety scares and more recently condemnation of the entire sector by an increasingly vocal environmental lobby. These protestors see the SUV as a gas-guzzling monster whose rightful place is in a field or a forest, and which definitely has no right to be on an urban street.

Such protests have, in places, reached religious levels, even spawning a popular US-based anti-SUV website entitled 'What Would Jesus Drive', but the evidence of the showrooms suggests very clearly that the SUV is here to stay. How this situation has come about is a complex story, stretching from the earliest spartan 4x4 machines to today's vehicles which are nothing short of executive cars, boasting all manner of creature comforts but also having the rather useful extra ability to turn off the blacktop and head off into the landscape.

The first question to pose is quite simply, what is an SUV? But this is quite difficult to answer. Basically there is no 'Eureka Moment' in the history of the SUV. There has never been a big motor show unveiling before hushed ranks of journalists, no company CEO announcing to the assembled media that 'this is our new model and we're creating a whole new type of car here, one which we have decided to call the Sports-Utility Vehicle.' Instead, the SUV evolved over several decades – there is not even any hard and fast evidence as to who first coined the term that is so familiar today. Arguments still rage as to which was the first SUV – rival proponents putting forward contenders ranging from vehicles manufactured from the 1930s to the 1980s.

Today it is generally accepted that SUVs are tough-looking, high-slung vehicles, usually – but not exclusively – boasting four-wheel-drive to give them serious off-road ability. The modern SUV also boasts exactly the same level of equipment that you would expect to find in a typical car, and has moved a long way away from the more basic workhorse 4x4 that initiated the SUV story. To show how that happened, and how a niche vehicle aimed at the military and farmers has become a mainstream line that no manufacturer can afford to do without, is the purpose of this book.

Most observers believe that the SUV as a distinct class of vehicle first emerged in the 1970s, but to explore the genesis of these unique automobiles we have to travel much further back in motoring history, to the mid-1930s in fact. Our story begins in the country where much of it will unfold: the United States of America. In the years after World War I even the financial hardship that followed the Wall Street Crash could not prevent America's love affair with the automobile from flourishing. Each year companies such as Chevrolet, Chrysler and of course Ford introduced more and more of the American public to the joys of motoring, but the mainstream vehicles, epitomized by Ford's Model-T, did not suit everyone. Out on the plains and in the hills of the rural USA such machines would not last five minutes – what roads that existed were rough-shod, some little more than tracks, and the vehicles that used them had to be tough enough to cope. This was the land of the truck – basic, spartan creations designed primarily to transport people and their goods from one place

1946 Jeep CJ-2A

Engine:

In-line 4-cyl petrol

Capacity:

2199cc (134.2ci)

Power:

60hp

Transmission:

3-speed manual, selectable 4WD

Construction:

Body-on-frame

Suspension:

Leaf springs all round

Brakes:

Drums all round

Weight:

3125lb (1417kg)

Top speed:

55mph (88.5kph)

0-60mph (97kph):

Not published

to another, with little or no attention paid to adding creature comforts.

At this time vehicle manufacturers were still learning what would sell and what would not. In the early 1920s a whole host of experiments had taken place, various body designs were fitted to both car and truck chassis and in the process what would become known as the station wagon was created. Aimed at increasing a vehicle's ability to carry both people and cargo, the station wagon extended the passenger compartment over the rear deck, adding more seats and a vertical deck lid below a rear window. These shells were made of wood and initially produced by specialist body builders, but in 1923 Durant, one of the founder companies of General Motors, built its own shell. The resultant vehicle was called the Star and it was effectively the first mainstream station wagon. By 1929 Ford was offering a similar design, and as more manufacturers followed suit the resultant models were dubbed 'Suburbans' or 'Carryalls'. One of these two words would usually appear in the model name, no matter which maker had produced the vehicle.

Chevrolet took the next big step, in 1934 putting on sale a vehicle that mounted a steel station wagon body on a truck chassis. Aimed at the army, it was called the 'Carryall-Suburban' and a sister General Motors Corporation (GMC) version was on sale by 1937, the first of what would be a long model line which is still on sale today. GMC advertising described the vehicle as 'ideal for use as a passenger vehicle or for transporting varied loads... Easily converted by removing quick-fastening seats.' Before long the Carryall-Suburban had spawned a range of variants, some for example being fitted with drop-down tailgates and others with double rear doors. At this stage, however, only two-wheel-drive transmission was offered.

At the outbreak of World War II, Dodge joined the Carryall game with its own steel-bodied station wagon, again pitched at military use but boasting four-wheel-drive, greatly increasing its versatility as it was far more assured where the blacktop ran out. After hostilities ended Dodge progressed its design into pick-up trucks, moving away from passenger

carrying, but Chevrolet persisted with its Suburban and by 1956 had added four-wheel-drive, effectively creating the first of what today are many claimants to the title of the first SUV.

Meanwhile World War II had seen the creation of a vehicle that was to play a pivotal role in the evolution of the SUV. Several machines have been credited as 'helping to win the war' and standing proud alongside such icons as the Spitfire fighter plane, Flying Fortress bomber and Sherman tank is the Willys-Jeep. A small and extremely basic four-wheel-drive off-roader, it was created as the result of a 1940 appeal from the US military to American car makers. Realizing they were about to get involved in the hostilities then going on in Europe and North Africa, the US Army demanded the creation of a fast four-wheel-drive off-road scout car – and they wanted prototypes running within 75 days. Established automobile manufacturers Ford and Willys-Overland answered the call but both found themselves beaten by the tiny American Bantam Car Company. Bantam had first attempted to build an army scout car in the 1930s and its new design impressed the military top brass the most.

Below: The Jeep made its name as the military workhorse of World War II. Examples were shipped all around the globe.

Above: No sooner was the
Jeep modified to suit civilian
use, than a Station Wagon
version was offered. Both
models are seen here.

Civilian Jeep

Once hostilities ended, Ford abandoned its Jeep production and went back to making cars. The blue oval badge would not return to this sector for some two decades. Willys-Overland, however, was more far-sighted. Facing the prospect of plummeting military orders in a post-war world, Willys Chief Engineer Barney Roos had an idea for a potential new market for his Jeeps. Even as the last campaigns were fought in the Pacific, Bantam's designers were busy modifying the Jeep's design to suit civilian use, Roos having visions of as many farmers driving his vehicles as had soldiers. Launched in August 1945 at a price of £600 ($1090), the new version was designated the CJ-2A, for 'Civilian Jeep' – CJ-1A had been applied to the 22 prototypes. It was clearly based on the military vehicle, and boasted distinguishing features that remain on Jeeps to this day – principally the seven-slat front grille and squared-off wheel arches.

Initial power for the CJ was provided by a four-cylinder engine of 2.2 litres (134.2 cubic inches) producing 60hp. The four-wheel-drive system was part-time, switched in from the normal rear-wheel-drive mode through a transfer case. Within a year a station wagon version appeared – the seed that three decades later would spawn one of the best-known SUVs, the Jeep Cherokee. Initially offered in two-wheel-drive only, the 4WD version launching in 1949, the Jeep Station Wagon was designed to look just like the wood-framed vehicles offered by the likes of Ford and General Motors, except that the effect was courtesy of a two-tone paint scheme – its frames were actually made from pressed steel. Jeep's advertising described the Station Wagon as 'a really new kind of car... a roomy, comfortable passenger car and a utility vehicle too'. The Station Wagon would stay in production for some 17 years with the only major change being an updating of its six-cylinder 2425cc (148ci) engine.

Takeovers and rivalry

The Jeep Station Wagon proved a big success, and versions of it were even built in Japan by Mitsubishi and Nissan, the latter then using the Datsun brand. Meanwhile the potential of Willys was noted by rival manufacturer Kaiser. In 1953 Kaiser paid £33 million ($60 million) to take over the firm, and the Jeeps became Kaiser-Jeeps. One of the first was an all-new model, the CJ-5, again based on a military vehicle and featuring a new 'Super Hurricane' six-cylinder engine and crucially a more rounded, better-looking body shell. Soon a bigger version followed, extending the 81-inch (2057mm) wheelbase to 101 inches (2565mm). With an extensive options list the CJ-5 models played a major role in establishing the Jeep as a recreational vehicle.

Meanwhile the ongoing success of the Station Wagon had resulted in Jeep acquiring a new rival built by a firm rather better known for making tractors and agricultural equipment. International Harvester (IH) had marketed a wooden-bodied carryall type vehicle for some time, calling it the Travelall. In 1957 it appeared with a steel body and four-wheel-drive, the posters presenting it as a vehicle that farming families could head to town in as well as driving across their fields. It was a successful move for IH and throughout the next two decades the company would play a significant role in the fledgling SUV market.

Kaiser's next move was to replace the Jeep Station Wagon. The new model appeared in late 1962, this being the first time a Jeep had been designed without military requirements taking top priority. It was offered in two-wheel and four-wheel-drive, and pick-up and station wagon form, and the latter gained a snazzy name, dubbed the Wagoneer. Launched in 1962, this is another vehicle that some today claim was one of the earliest Sports-Utility Vehicles – it was aimed squarely at outdoor types who spent their weekends in the countryside enjoying pastimes such as fishing or hunting. It looked like a chunky car, and Jeep's own advertising talked of 'passenger car styling with the advantages of four-wheel-drive'.

Above: 1955 saw the launch of the Jeep CJ-5, boasting a more shapely body and a six-cylinder engine that boosted the model's status in the recreational market.

Below: The Jeep Wagoneer was an early attempt to close the gap between the workhorse 4x4 and the family car, and as a result some claim it was the first true SUV.

The Wagoneer used the new Tornado six-cylinder overhead-cam truck engine and within four years it had been joined by a V8 version, followed swiftly by the Super Wagoneer. This was pitched more upmarket, with such car-like features as a vinyl roof and three-tone paintwork. These model lines would last for many years and with many increases in engine sizes, a 5.9-litre (360ci) V8 being among the most notable power options.

Back in its earliest post-war years Jeep had briefly marketed a small two-wheel-drive model, the Jeepster. The company's final act of the 1960s was to revive the concept in 4WD form. Alongside the pick-up and convertible versions was offered a two-door station wagon, called the Jeepster Commando. The standard engine was the four-cylinder Hurricane with a Dauntless V6 on the options list. Crucially, it was also the first small 4WD vehicle to include automatic transmission on the options list. Jeep was well prepared for the rise of the SUV – but the company also now faced growing competition, in particular a new rival from across the Atlantic Ocean.

To pick up this strand of the SUV time-line we return to 1947, a period when thousands of pensioned-off wartime Jeeps were being adapted to new civilian uses all over the western world. One of these had ended up at a farm on the island of Anglesey, off the coast of Wales. The farm was owned by Maurice Wilks, chief designer of the Rover car company and he found the US machine very useful for getting about his fields. But for both business and patriotic reasons, reliance on the US machine did not sit easily with Maurice.

After six years building military hardware Rover's factories were now largely idle. Maurice's brother Spencer, Managing Director of the firm, was keen to get back to car manufacture, but was hamstrung like much of British industry by a severe shortage of steel. Both men knew that in order for the company to survive until steel supplies became easier to obtain they needed a 'stop-gap' design that used rather less of the precious metal.

The story goes that while charging across his fields and pondering the problem, Maurice wore out his Jeep and complained to Spencer that the only thing he could replace it with was another Jeep as there was no British equivalent. Immediately the two saw Rover's salvation, a simple, tough, 4x4 vehicle aimed at agricultural use – the Land Rover.

The first prototypes, using a very basic body mounted over the mechanics of Rover's P3 car, were already running by the time Spencer floated the Land Rover proposal to Rover's board in September 1947. Development was swift, basically because Rover's workforce desperately needed something to build, and the first production Land Rover was duly unveiled to the public at the Amsterdam Motor Show in April 1948. In many ways it was like the Jeep. Rover had actually acquired two of the American vehicles at an early stage of the design process and dismantled them, but the designers argued that the final British machine was distinctly different, particularly in the way that it used existing Rover parts wherever possible. Chief among these was the engine, Rover's newest 1595cc (97ci) unit eventually chosen for its extra power, a total of 50hp, over the 1.4 used in the prototypes. Yet it was still a much smaller engine than that used in the Jeep, allowing the Land Rover to boast more carrying space.

Above: In the late 1960s Jeep revived the concept of a smaller 4x4 with the Jeepster. The model pictured here is the station wagon version, known as the Commando.

Left: The Jeepster was also offered in traditional pick-up form and as a convertible, seen here. Among the options was an automatic transmission, the first offered on a small 4x4.

decades later. Part of this was due to the fact that if you could prove your Land Rover was a commercial vehicle and not a private car, it was exempt from purchase tax and could use cheaper 'pink' fuel.

In 1952 Land Rover tried again with the seven-seater station wagon and a cheaper, more basic version proved more successful. By now Land Rovers were flying out of the factory in Solihull near Birmingham and design changes came thick and fast as the company struggled to keep up with sales orders. More rear space was a major demand, so in 1954 the 80-inch version was extended to 86 inches (2184mm) and a new long-wheelbase Land Rover, the 107-inch (2718mm), launched alongside. Within two years these grew to 88 and 109 inches

Above: Land Rover quickly followed Jeep's lead by producing a seven-seat station wagon, but the 1948 version was overpriced and did not sell in large numbers.

Initially the Land Rover was nothing but a pure workhorse. It had an 80-inch (2032mm) wheelbase, an open pick-up body style (though a fabric hood with perspex windows could be added), full-time four-wheel-drive and lots of power take-offs allowing it to drive machinery. It went on sale for just £450, though for that you got the very basic vehicle – even a cushion for the passenger seat was on the options list, as were doors! As Rover's salesmen learned more about their new market the doors made it onto the standard equipment list. The Land Rover proved an immediate success, selling 3048 in the first year and initially taking full advantage of its exemption from a post-war austerity rule that allowed customers to buy only one new car every two years. By the end of 1948 a second version with a hardtop was on sale, built around a new light alloy shell and featuring a pair of inward-facing seats on each side of the load bay. This allowed the Land Rover to carry seven passengers but crippling UK purchase tax inflated the price of this model to double that of the open version and it sold poorly, lasting only to 1951.

This proved only a minor setback – by 1951 Rover was selling two Land Rovers to every car. The vehicles were being used for a far wider range of applications than their original farm intentions and several soon found their way onto the road, effectively foreshadowing the rise of the SUV

Right: Land Rover's sales success quickly spawned more variants – this promotional shot shows short- and long-wheelbase canvas top versions and a long-wheelbase station wagon.

Left: Land Rover's station wagon featured a side-opening tailgate, while the rear seats faced inward towards each other, making it capable of carrying seven.

(2235 and 2769mm) to accommodate the first diesel engines in the Land Rover range. Customers demanded a diesel powerplant but Rover had never made one in its history. A new engine was duly designed but it proved to be too large for the Land Rover's engine bay, so the simple solution was to make the vehicle bigger.

Below: The extension of the Land Rover wheelbase to 107 inches greatly suited the station wagon application, as shown in this Series I example.

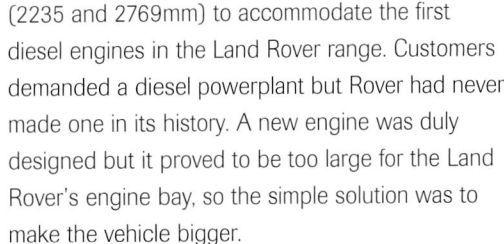

The result of these changes was known as the Land Rover Series II. The petrol-engined version gained a new powerplant too, a 2.3-litre (139.4ci) unit offering the same 52hp as the new 2.0-litre (125ci) diesel but more torque – 101lb/ft compared to the diesel's 87lb/ft. Before long both engines would be producing more than 70hp. The chassis was updated and some minor body restyling carried out, while other changes included proper glass side windows instead of perspex ones.

The introduction of the Land Rover Series II was timely as rival UK manufacturer Austin was now trying to steal some of the market with its new Gipsy, a lightweight, Jeep-like vehicle. This was a successor to the Champ, which had been aimed squarely at the Army but never progressed much beyond the basic model. Similarly the Gipsy was never developed to anything like the level of the Land Rover, while within a short time a serious corrosion problem emerged and fatally damaged its reputation. It did attract some sales and was exported to both the USA and Canada, but would eventually disappear in 1968 when Austin and Land Rover both became part of the British Leyland conglomerate. It was uneconomical for one

company to produce two competing vehicles and unsurprisingly it was the Land Rover that the new management went for.

The Land Rover Series II was launched at a price of £640 for the petrol-powered 88-inch (2235mm) version, and £730 for the long-wheelbase variant, and in its first year more than 28,000 units were sold. Land Rover was now selling so many vehicles that it faced a new problem. In the UK the public and some media commentators were now referring to any 4x4 vehicle, no matter who it was made by, as a land rover. Everyone that is except the BBC, which anxious not to contravene its 'no-advertising' rules, used the previous popular term Jeep in its broadcasts! This went on until Land Rover's management pointed out to the BBC exactly what a Jeep was. By now the British sales success included the export market, and vehicles sold all over the world including in the Jeep stronghold of North America. Since 1956 Spanish company Santana had also been making Land Rovers under licence, exporting them to 25 countries including parts of Central and South America.

At around this time Land Rover's design department carried out some research on a vehicle

that – had it made it into production – could have been a true early SUV. The brief was to combine the simple shell of the Land Rover with some of the comforts of a typical car. Dubbed the 'Road Rover' this project has been identified by some as the forerunner of the Range Rover, but Spen King, who would design the later model, has dismissed the Road Rover as a mere experiment, pointing out for example that it was never planned to boast four-wheel-drive. Dogged by the lack of either a suitable chassis or sufficient funding, the Road Rover project progressed only as far as some prototype vehicles; the first was angular and ugly and nicknamed 'The Greenhouse'. By 1958 the project was dead but no doubt some in the company never forgot the potential for a more road-friendly Land Rover.

By the end of the 1950s Jeep, Chevrolet and International Harvester in America, and Land Rover in Britain, had established a significant 4x4 sector,

but the rise of the SUV was still some time away. In the next few years these three companies would find themselves in competition with familiar rivals as other more mainstream manufacturers turned their attention to this popular type of vehicle. But all would also face a serious and rapidly growing challenge from a new direction – the Far East.

Above: Despite the rise of the recreational 4x4, the Land Rover's prime application remained as a workhorse. Here it is being promoted as suitable for airport duties.

2 A New Challenge from the East

While Jeep and Land Rover had dominated the growth of 4x4s in the west, in the east a sleeping giant was stirring. Today Toyota is not only Japan's biggest car manufacturer but a major global player in the Sports-Utility Vehicle sector with a long history of making 4x4s. Like Land Rover, the start of this story involved the Jeep.

Above: A truck manufacturing contract for the US Army provided Toyota with the hardware to create this vehicle, known as the BJ, which was effectively the first Land Cruiser.

Toyota's Land Cruiser celebrated its 50th anniversary in 2001 but this apparent milestone is not quite what it seems – the first version of what would become one of the most recognizable SUVs across the globe was a very humble machine that struggled for buyers. Launched in Japan in 1951 as the Toyota BJ, the first Land Cruiser looked very much like the Jeeps then in use by the American military forces occupying the country following World War II. In fact much of its mechanicals were sourced from a truck contract that Toyota was completing for the US Army. Toyota hoped that Japan's own military requirements would produce lots of sales for the BJ and even demonstrated the model's prowess by driving one a long way up Mount Fuji, far beyond the point where any previous motor vehicle had been. This was all the more impressive when you considered that the 3386cc (206.5ci) six-cylinder 85hp engine's 4x4 transmission had no low-range gearing. But Japan's

soldiers opted instead for Jeeps, which by that time were being built in the country under licence by rival manufacturer Mitsubishi.

In the next two years Toyota sold fewer than 300 BJ models, so in 1954 a new version was launched, the 20 Series. Its wheelbase was shortened from 95 (2413mm) to 90 inches (2286mm) and a new and more shapely body was added, with steel doors replacing the canvas versions

of its predecessor. To coincide with the new model going into mass production, Toyota coined the name Land Cruiser. By 1958 it was finding success in export markets – the Japanese had always had an eye on exports: the 20 Series instrument panel and glovebox were identically shaped to ensure that left- or right-hand-drive versions could equally easily be made. Toyota also varied wheelbase lengths and body styles to suit the market targeted, using the Land Cruiser to open up the sector and then following on with their passenger cars. 1958 saw the model launched in the United States, coinciding with the unveiling of the first of the hard-top versions. Jeep, which had successfully prevented the first Land Cruiser from being a success in Japan, now found the new rival competing in its own back yard as Toyota taught US and European motor manufacturers a lesson in export strategy.

By 1961 the Land Cruiser was the best-selling Toyota in America, but the biggest boost came four years later. The 40 Series Land Cruiser was unveiled in 1964 and immediately gained a reputation as an extremely tough vehicle. In 1965 it was joined by the 50 Series, a station wagon that offered just what many Americans were looking for. It was based on a 40 with its wheelbase extended by almost two inches (50mm). Its six-cylinder 3.9-litre (238ci) engine was tuned to offer more high-end power, totalling 125hp, for better highway cruising, and everything was wrapped in a much more elegant body and fitted with all the creature comforts expected of a typical car. This was effectively a true SUV, and it was an immediate hit, evidenced by the fact that Toyota sold its 100,000th Land Cruiser worldwide in 1968, yet had doubled that figure just four years later and passed 300,000 a year after that.

Above: 1964 saw Toyota unveiling the Land Cruiser 40 Series, a vehicle that was as tough as it was stylish. Like Series I Land Rovers, many '40s' are still running today.

Left: The Land Cruiser 40 Series appealed to many buyers outside the traditional workhorse market, thanks to such styling touches as its smooth corners and wraparound rear windows.

Above: While Toyota produced newer Land Cruiser lines, the 40 Series would go on and on, eventually surviving more than 20 years into the mid-1980s.

Helping to keep these figures growing was constant development of the model line, including new engine sizes and power outputs, but the clearest evidence of the growing importance of the SUV-style 4x4 came in 1980. While the 40 Series was still going strong and would do so until 1985, a replacement for the 50 Series was revealed. The 60 Series boasted new petrol and diesel engines, third-row seats and even more luxuries – on-road performance clearly greatly influenced its design, though the essential off-road ability remained courtesy of its solid axles and lockable differentials front and rear.

Toyota, however, was not the only Japanese manufacturer rising to global prominence. Rival Nissan had followed a very similar path when creating its first 4x4. Like Toyota's BJ this was launched in 1951, though Nissan's vehicle, called the 4W-60 and the first of what would become the 60 series, was the product of a deal to build Jeeps under licence. Naturally it looked very much like the Willys-Jeep, but Nissan's version boasted one significant difference – under its bonnet sat not a four-cylinder motor but 3.2 litres (195ci) of six-cylinder truck engine. Its 84 horsepower was 25 more than the Jeep offered, which made it very popular in its home market, and by the time exports reached America in 1961 the Nissan was pushing out 125 horses. It was still very basic, however, a trait Nissan rectified in 1960 with a new shell, interior and name – Patrol.

The Patrol was not exported in huge numbers, but those Americans who got their hands on one were amazed by its abilities. With its three-speed transmission, two-speed reduction gears and stabilized front suspension, the Patrol could tackle most conditions thrown at it, including fording rivers more than two feet deep. Soon an optional hard top

Right: The 50 Series cemented Toyota's growing reputation. Based on an extended 40 Series, this model, introduced in 1965, was effectively a true SUV, and an immediate hit.

added to the Patrol's versatility, while by the mid-1970s station wagon versions had joined the range anticipating later true SUVs. The first Patrol line would last until 1982, with 170,000 eventually being built.

A third Japanese manufacturer would soon carve itself a slice of the SUV pie, but its models were rather different from those of Toyota or Nissan. Suzuki's name was already widely known, but among fans of two-wheeled propulsion, not four. The company's motorcycles were widely renowned, and not surprisingly its first car of 1955 was powered by a two-stroke motorcycle engine. In 1968 Suzuki began work on what would eventually become a very successful small SUV line, buying the manufacturing rights to a compact and very basic 4x4 from struggling fellow Japanese maker the Hope Motor Company. The Suzuki LJ launched in Japan in 1970, the letters standing for 'Light Jeep' because that is exactly what it was, a basic 4x4 very similar to the Jeep. It was a tiny vehicle, just 118 inches (2997mm) long to fit into Japan's microcar regulations, while the mere 1323lb (600kg) weight ensured the motorcycle powerplant, producing just 25hp, was not over-stretched. You could buy 'Brute' or 'Jimny' versions, the latter name reputedly coined after a Suzuki party visited Scotland and mis-heard the slang-phrase 'Jimmy!'

The Suzuki soon found a niche, below the Jeep and Land Rover, as a small, fun vehicle. Soon exports were flying out to Australia and from 1978 to Britain. Farmers loved its small size, enabling them to use it on tracks and bridleways too small for Land Rovers, but Suzuki's UK importer soon recognized a new market. Newspaper adverts headed 'Wild Weekender' alerted urban dwellers to the weekend thrill of off-road driving, highlighting the machine's versatility and particularly its transmission, which could be turned from two-wheel- to four-wheel-drive at the flick of a switch.

By the time it reached Britain the SJ had been seriously developed beyond the early basic versions. The canvas hoods of the early vehicles soon made way for proper steel bodies that included a station wagon version. By the time of the UK launch the engines had grown too – power now came from a conventional 797cc (48.6ci) four-stroke unit offering 40hp.

Above: Launched in 1980, the Land Cruiser 60 Series had the look and feel of today's SUV, boasting plenty of creature comforts and much improved on-road performance.

Below: One of Toyota's prime home rivals was Nissan. The latter's Patrol, launched in 1960, proved as equally long-lasting as the Land Cruiser.

Right: Chevrolet's Blazer first appeared in 1969, and was effectively little more than a pick-up truck with a glassfibre hard top bolted on to create a pseudo-station wagon.

1969 Chevrolet Blazer

Engine:

V8 petrol

Capacity:

5735cc (350ci)

Power:

165hp

Transmission:

3-speed manual/auto, selectable 4WD

Construction:

Body-on-frame

Suspension:

Leaf springs all round

Brakes:

Front disc, rear drum

Weight:

5157lb (2339kg)

Top speed:

98mph (158kph)

0-60mph (97kph):

15.0 seconds

Angled at America

Having secured its place in the market, Suzuki exploited it with the new SJ. It was longer and wider than the LJ, built around a new chassis and fitted for export with a new 970cc (59ci) 45hp engine. The model also marked the debut of the angular body styling that became the hallmark of the Suzuki range. With this model Suzuki felt confident of attacking the American market, but faced a difficulty it had already experienced in Britain – a very restrictive import quota on Japanese vehicles

imposed by the US government. The answer was to sign a deal with General Motors, which in 1982 would lead to the launch of the S10 Chevrolet Blazer, the second Chevy to carry the Blazer name.

The first Chevrolet Blazer had appeared a decade earlier as General Motors took a greater interest in the fledgling SUV market. GM's mainstay through the 1960s had been its Suburban Carryalls as rival manufacturers dropped away – only Dodge persisted with a vehicle called the Town Wagon. This lasted until 1966, with styling virtually unchanged

Right: Chevrolet and GMC were sister companies, so it was no surprise that GMC's Jimmy, launched in 1970, was to all intents and purposes a Chevy Blazer wearing a different badge.

from its launch year of 1958 and with annual sales in the mere hundreds. GMC would finally register the terms Suburban and Carryall as trademarks in 1988, but in 1970 it began to experiment in a new direction with what has been dubbed its first SUV.

Based on a pick-up truck called the C/K, the new model launched as the Chevrolet Blazer in 1969 and the GMC Jimmy in 1970. While seemingly anticipating the later tie-up with Suzuki by correcting the Japanese company's spelling mistake, the Jimmy actually recalled an earlier GMC military truck line. Power came from a six-cylinder four-litre (250ci) engine offering 110hp, while the options list included a 4.7-litre (292ci) version of 125hp, and two V8s pushing power up to a maximum of 170hp. Two-wheel-drive was offered, though few were sold in this form. There was no station wagon but instead a completely lift-off glassfibre body, and this survived through a major facelift in 1973. A steel half-cab arrived in 1976, while by the 1980s a diesel had joined the engine line-up. But there was still no proper station wagon.

What, however, of Jeep, the marque that had done so much to create the SUV market? The Wagoneer, Super Wagoneer and the Jeepster Commando maintained Jeep's presence into the 1970s, the start of which saw major changes in the company. In February 1970 £5.6 million ($10 million) saw Kaiser-Jeep swallowed up by the American Motors Corporation, and the new owners immediately divided the company in two. The military lines moved to a former Studebaker plant in Indiana, leaving the plant in Toledo, Ohio to produce civilian Jeeps under the name of AMC. Apart from that, there was little change to the Jeep line. The Commando was restyled but by 1973 it had been dropped, while more basic versions of the Wagoneer were introduced, dubbed the Cherokee and Cherokee Chief. As the decade progressed the Wagoneer range was steadily improved, the most notable update was a new full-time four-wheel-drive system for the automatic gearboxes dubbed Quadra-Trac, the descendent of which is found in today's Jeep models.

Below: Jeep first used the model name Cherokee on a more basic version of the Wagoneer launched in 1973. It was not until years later that the name became a Jeep signature line.

Above: The Renegade was a new model to Jeep, introduced in 1974 and designed as an upmarket fun vehicle.

Below: Among the range of Renegade variants was this 1970s van design.

New to the Jeep line in 1974 was the Renegade, an upmarket model, stretching the stock CJ5's wheelbase from 81 (2057mm) to almost 84 inches (2134mm) to allow fitting of the new straight-six engine that AMC had introduced in 1972. The Renegade also offered two V8 engines, while transmission choices included three- and four-speed manuals and an automatic. The CJ5 was

effectively replaced in 1976 by the CJ7 (though the older model would still be built until 1983), and the new model's car-style doors and one-piece removable hardtop made of injection-moulded plastic proved popular with buyers. The wheelbase grew again, to 93.4 inches (2372mm), as Jeep aimed squarely at the recreational SUV market – chrome trim was applied liberally and the rapidly extending options list included such desirables as radio players and air conditioning.

In fact, while no-one at the Ohio factory realized it at the time, the most significant event to affect Jeep in the 1970s was when French manufacturer Renault, desperate to break into the American market, purchased half of AMC in 1979. This move would, within a few years, lead to the creation of the most significant Jeep model yet. Something dramatic was needed, because by the end of the 1970s Jeep had slipped from market leader to a bit player in the SUV story.

In fact many believe that Jeep's other home-grown competitor, International Harvester, had kicked the growth of SUVs into gear back in 1961

when it built a companion to its Travelall, calling its new creation the Scout. This is yet another vehicle that stakes a claim to the title of first SUV, and its success is pinpointed by some observers as the defining moment that persuaded the giants of Ford, GM and Chrysler to seriously enter the fray. The Scout, with a 2490cc (152ci) four-cylinder 93hp powerplant and either two- or four-wheel-drive, was intended to rival the Jeep directly. By 1967 it had been updated, a V8 had joined the range and variety was the watchword, as this extract from an early advertisement makes clear:

'One man lives halfway up a mountain – he wants his Scout with all-wheel drive, a V8 engine and four-on-the-floor. He's got it. Another drives his to work, on nice, flat blacktop (tarmac). He'll take a 4 or maybe a 6-cylinder engine with a simple stick shift or an automatic... and only two-wheel drive. OK! One uses his Scout like a pickup. He gets a cab top. Another Scout is somebody's second car. Full length Traveltop with rear seats for him. How much Scout do you need?'

A completely new version, the Scout II, emerged in 1972 and this was far closer to today's accepted image of an SUV. The body styling was more user-friendly and the interior boasted such niceties as vinyl seat coverings. The Scout II came with six engine choices ranging from a four-cylinder 3211cc (196ci) to a six-cylinder 5653cc (345ci) and three- and four-speed manual gearboxes along with an automatic. It would last until 1980, eventually becoming a victim of a cash crisis at International Harvester. As an interesting sideline, IH was one of the first manufacturers to react to the environmental damage caused by off-roading 4x4 owners, a problem that would become one of the environmental lobby's main weapons to attack the whole SUV sector in coming decades. In October 1978, IH launched its 'Take a Stand to Save the Land' policy. Its aim was to encourage 4x4 owners to drive with some thought for the landscape they were traversing.

The success of the Scout, and the continuing sales enjoyed by Jeep and Land Rover, did not go unnoticed by the giants of the US motor industry.

GM had entered the contest with its Blazer/Jimmy range, but the clearest indication that this was now a serious market sector had come in 1965 when Ford launched its first SUV. The model was the Bronco, and it was aimed squarely at the Jeep CJ-5 and Scout. Following GM's lead, Ford took a truck chassis as the basis for the newcomer, initially producing a spartan machine powered by a six-cylinder 2785cc (170ci) 105hp engine already familiar to drivers of Ford's Falcon. Like its rivals Ford offered the Bronco in open, half cab and station wagon varieties, but the open version sold badly and was dropped within three years – a sure sign of changing emphasis in the market.

Above: Jeep advertising of the 1970s emphasized the fun aspect of their vehicles – even on the sales lot! The presence of young, attractive buyers in the picture was also considered to be highly desirable.

Below: Jeep's Renegade could be bought with a bolt-on hardtop made from injection moulded plastic, the closest this particular model ever came to being an SUV.

Right: Ford's first entry into the 4x4 recreational vehicle sector was dubbed the Bronco. As this picture shows, it was based squarely on a truck.

Below: Ford aimed to appeal to the entire market with open, half-cab, and station wagon versions of the Bronco, but the open model was dropped within three years of its launch.

Within a year of launch a 4735cc (289ci) V8 engine had joined the line-up and Ford was learning quickly about this new market. A Sport version was soon on offer, boasting a range of styling options to attract the increasing leisure users of 4x4s. By the early 1970s the base engine was a 3.2-litre (200ci) unit while the V8 had grown to almost five litres (302ci), but the arrival of Chevrolet's Blazer and the IH Scout II soon left Ford's contender in their wake. The blue oval did not exactly help its case either – neither auto transmission nor power steering could be found on the Bronco options list until 1973.

Major changes were needed and Ford's answer was the first of the 'full-size' Broncos, the second generation, which made its appearance in 1978 and remained in production for a whole two years. In fact it had been planned for launch in 1973 but the oil crisis in the Middle East resulted in serious fuel shortages across the globe, and little enthusiasm for a gas-guzzling V8 SUV like the Bronco. When the new model finally appeared, with a rather more environmentally friendly engine alongside the V8 units, it was much praised. Based on Ford's F-Series pick-up truck, the Bronco was tough, with all the off-road ability one expected of a 4x4, but it also came with a wide range of creature comforts, such as air conditioning and cruise control – there was even a Ranger XLT model aimed directly at the family driver.

The Bronco stormed to the top of sales charts and swept car of the year awards across America,

but fatally it had appeared too late. The delays in the second-generation Bronco's launch had pushed it back into competition with the third-generation model that Ford was developing. Launched in 1980 this was the SUV of the future, designed to cope with energy worries and a less secure economy. Its base 4.9-litre (300ci) engine used less fuel, while the vehicle itself was lighter, cheaper to build and therefore to sell. Its designers also pointed squarely in the direction they saw SUVs heading – the new Bronco boasted not a solid front axle to suit the off-road set, but a 'twin traction-beam' unit that produced better manners on the blacktop. Ford knew what it was doing – this Bronco would stay in production for two decades.

Above: Ford's Bronco sold well initially but did not manage to keep pace with its rivals from both within America and the Far East.

Above left: Despite updates, by the time this 1977 model was launched the Bronco was lagging seriously behind the competition.

Left: Ford answered its critics with the new 'full-size' Bronco of 1978. It won car of the year awards on its launch but within only two years it had been replaced by a third-generation model.

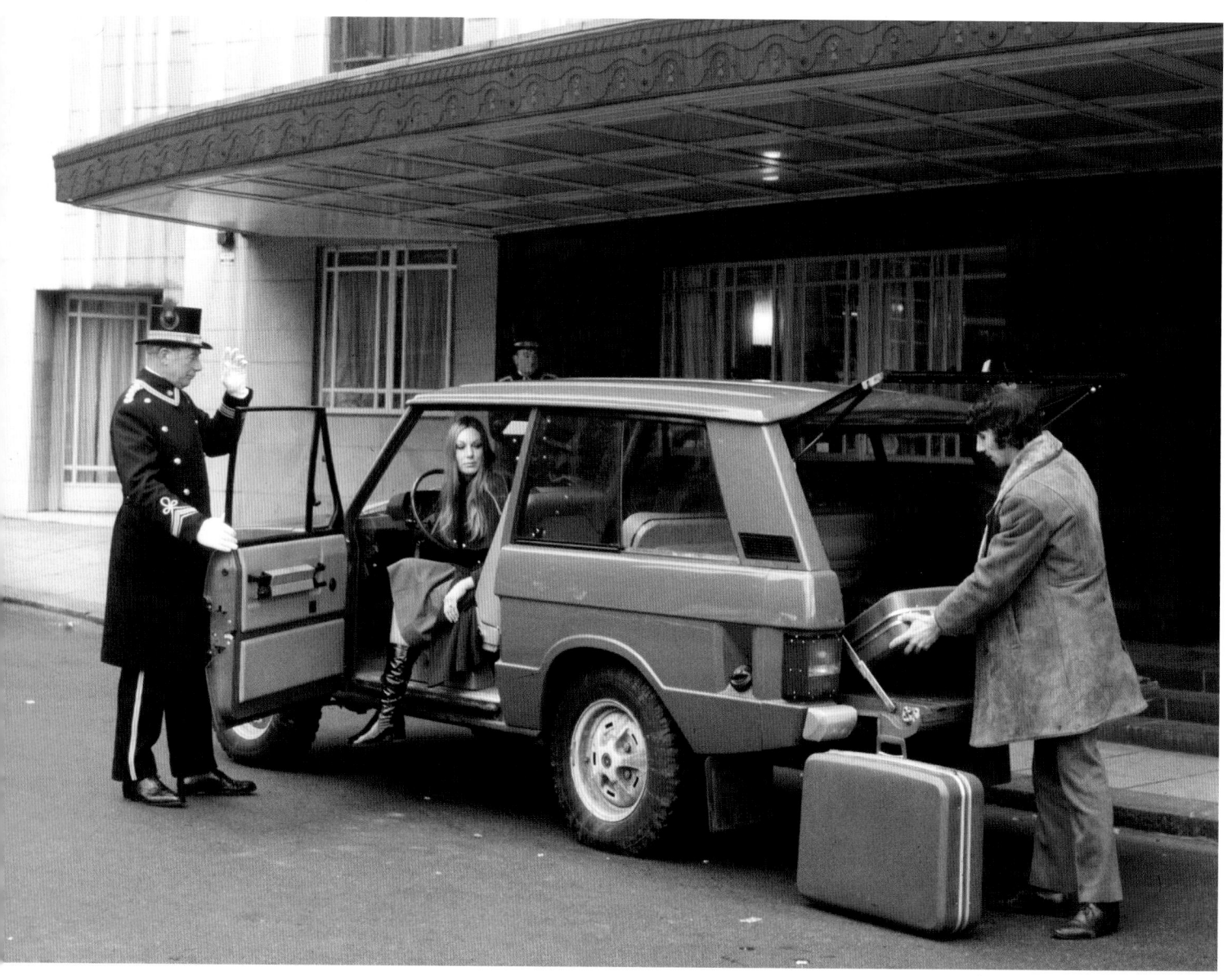

Above: This advertising shot from the 1970s leaves no doubt as to the type of buyer at which Land Rover bosses pitched their new Range Rover. Nevertheless, it was still very much a vehicle with serious off-road ability

A star is born!

Meanwhile across the Atlantic Land Rover had turned the SUV spotlight firmly on the UK with the unveiling in 1970 of the Range Rover, a vehicle that had all the off-road ability of its renowned sister vehicle but much more in the way of luxury. Boasting the level of equipment that buyers might expect to find in executive cars, the Range Rover was clearly aimed at more upmarket land owners, and those whose weekend diversions might involve hunting or shooting or towing a horse box to an equestrian event.

The concept of the Range Rover was actually born out of resistance to the idea of making the Land Rover less utilitarian. Management consistently rejected designers' proposals for softer springs and more comfortable interiors, arguing that the vehicle was a workhorse – nothing more. There was also a

degree of fear that matching a 4x4 off-road drivetrain to road speeds could produce a somewhat dangerous vehicle. However, by the 1960s evidence was growing (particularly in America) of a market for a more leisure pursuit-orientated, luxury version of the Land Rover, reviving the concept that had spawned the abortive Road Rover project of a decade earlier. Conveniently this came at a time when the market for military Land Rovers had declined.

A concept was undergoing tests by 1966. It used a new 135hp 3.5-litre (213ci) V8 engine which Rover had obtained from General Motors in the USA and was using in its P5 and P6 cars. It would make the Range Rover capable of almost 100mph (161kph), a speed unheard of in a four-wheel-drive vehicle. The permanent four-wheel-drive system gained a third differential, giving the newcomer excellent traction off-road. A new chassis was created around a 100-inch (254mm) wheelbase to provide a combination of off-road prowess and on-road refinement, and a two-door station wagon body was fitted along with an interior matching the quality standards of the P6. The highly recognizable body shape elicited wide-ranging praise – one would later become the first vehicle displayed at the Louvre art gallery in Paris, shown as an example of contemporary sculpture! The prototype was dubbed a Road Rover, but by 1968 the name Range Rover had been chosen.

By now Rover had been absorbed by Leyland and the new management saw the Range Rover as a high profile launch model for the company. It was revealed to the British public in 1970, initially priced at £2000. This was expensive for the time, but that simply added a desirability factor, and demand far exceeded Rover's wildest speculations. Everyone wanted a Range Rover, from wealthy farmers to traffic police officers. Buyers loved its performance, and they also enjoyed its raised seating position – not only when negotiating tricky cross-country routes but also when towering over fellow road users at traffic lights. This was something that would become a defining element of the SUV craze.

Despite some drawbacks, the 15mpg (19lit/ 100km) fuel economy figure being one of them, order books bulged and waiting lists grew very long. Some desperate customers even turned to a burgeoning black market, paying half as much again to get their hands on a Range Rover. Except, that is, in America, where stringent emissions regulations for many years dissuaded Leyland management from marketing their top model across the Atlantic.

Above: It was not until 1981 that an official four-door Range Rover went on sale, although before that date many vehicles were converted by aftermarket specialists.

Left: The launch of the Range Rover was a seminal moment in the SUV story, though its designers made an initial mistake by not adding a rear pair of doors.

Above: The Land Rover V8 of 1979 may have looked like a workhorse but its creators had one eye firmly on the leisure market, aiming it at those who desired a Range Rover but could not afford one.

One Range Rover feature that buyers did not like, however, was the lack of a second pair of doors. The designers had decided on two doors because they feared that fitting four might weaken a body that had to stand up to off-road use – though the cost factor was also a serious consideration. Throughout the 1970s a whole host of customized Range Rovers were made by independent specialists, and among the various limousines and even convertibles, the most popular was the one that added the extra doors. Eventually an official version appeared, but it took 11 years to arrive as the four-door Range Rover launched in 1981.

This might have been the time to allow the Range Rover to take over the SUV mantle, leaving Land Rover to concentrate on its core workhorse market, but in 1971, while struggling to keep pace with mushrooming Range Rover sales, Land Rover updated its core vehicle. The Series III was an

Right: The Land Rover V8's powerplant was sourced from the Range Rover but detuned by more than 40 horsepower.

evolution of the Series II – from the outside the only obvious difference on the new model was a redesigned radiator grille. The biggest mechanical alteration was a new all-synchromesh gearbox, but the interior came in for major changes, and the dashboard was completely redesigned.

Changing focus

Sales continued to flourish and in 1976 the Solihull factory built its one millionth Land Rover. Three years later it produced the first of a line that is central to our story, the V8 Land Rover. Applied to the 109-inch (2769mm) model, it used the drivetrain of the Range Rover, though with the motor detuned to 90.7hp. Its creators were clearly targeting the growing leisure 4x4 market, hoping to grab sales from those buyers who liked the Range Rover but simply couldn't afford it. Evidence of this were the V8's bright new colour scheme options, featuring names such as Inca Yellow and Pageant Blue.

By now Leyland had turned Land Rover into a standalone company, separating it from Rover Cars and pouring in £200 million of investment. The money paid for the creation of the four-door Range Rover, the V8 Land Rover and in 1982 the Land Rover County. This model, offered in both 89 (2261mm) and 109-inch (2769mm) formats, bridged the gap between Land Rover and Range Rover. Easily distinguished by its bright side stripes, the County boasted redesigned and adjustable seats upholstered in fabric rather than vinyl. Self-levelling suspension came as standard for a more comfortable ride, the interior was much more efficiently sound-proofed, and even such niceties as tinted glass added. Land Rover too, it seemed, could see exactly where the 4x4 market was heading – the age of the Sports-Utility Vehicle had finally arrived.

Above: While not as smoothly panelled as its Land Cruiser rival from the Far East, the Land Rover V8, pictured here in station wagon form, had plenty of carrying capacity.

Left: Crucially, the V8 also provided every ounce of off-road ability that had become the hallmark of all the vehicles that wore the Land Rover badge.

3 The Rise of the SUV

As the 1980s dawned, the SUV phenomenon was beginning to exert a serious influence across the globe, fed both by American manufacturers and the growing Japanese industry – Toyota had blazed a trail, Suzuki had followed suit and now other makers were looking for a slice of this business.

The two new major players were Nissan and Isuzu. The former, buoyed by the success of its Patrol, produced a new version in 1979. The Patrol 60 had always been a domestic model, though it had been exported and sold particularly well in South America. The new 160 was designed from the start to be an export model and within two years of its launch production had been expanded to a new factory in Spain.

The new Patrol could be purchased with either a 2.8-litre (170ci) 120hp diesel engine or a 3.3-litre (200ci) diesel with 95 horsepower. While its styling was still not very radical – the shell was a boxy unit without flowing, curvy lines – under the skin there were many advances. The diesel, for example boasted five speeds in its gearbox to make the most of the oil-burning engine's narrower power band

(the petrol variant gained five speeds in 1985). Power steering was offered, as was a lockable rear differential to cope with more extreme off-road conditions. It was designed to last a long time too – Nissan would keep it in production for a decade, though making constant updates to stay competitive in a now rapidly speeding-up SUV market.

A new name that entered the SUV market at around this time was Isuzu. It belonged to Japan's oldest car manufacturer, created way back in 1916 and named after a Japanese river. Isuzu made its first 4x4 in 1937, a seven-seater, but for many years this small firm's main contribution to the SUV market was in engines, particularly diesels – Isuzu motors were used by a number of manufacturers not only across Asia but in America and Australia. But the company's small size had always given it

Right: After years of providing engines for SUVs, Japan's oldest manufacturer Isuzu built its own, the Trooper.

problems and after abortive attempts to join up with fellow Japanese manufacturers Mitsubishi, Nissan and Subaru, in 1971 Isuzu sold 34 per cent of its stock to General Motors.

A decade later saw the launch of Isuzu's first entry into the SUV market. In Japan it was called the Bighorn, but it was built from the start for global export where it carried the rather more familiar title of Trooper. Initially launched as a two-door vehicle, the four-door followed a year later, and both immediately proved popular. Three petrol engines were offered ranging from 1949cc (119ci) to 2559cc (156ci) and 88 to 111hp, and not surprisingly a pair of diesels, the more powerful 2771cc (169ci) version putting 95hp through its five-speed manual transmission. The four-wheel-drive was permanent although, after 1987, modifications allowed the front-end to be

disengaged – a limited slip differential was also offered on the rear axle from this year. Vitally the Trooper came with lots of creature comforts and proved popular, even in America where the Trooper became yet another thorn in the side of the home-grown SUV manufacturers.

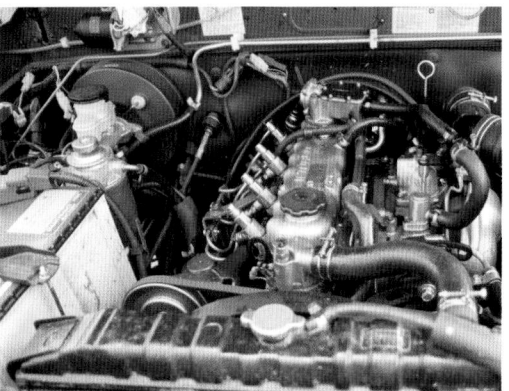

Above: The Isuzu Trooper was a competent entry into the SUV market and found plenty of buyers right across the globe.

Left: From the start Isuzu offered several engine options in the Trooper: three petrol units and a pair of its well-proven diesels.

Right: Toyota replaced its long-running Land Cruiser 40 Series with the 70 Series, which launched in 1984 and was essentially aimed at those who needed a vehicle for work.

Below: The Land Cruiser 70 Series was built for tough conditions, with a ladder frame and leaf springs as standard.

The Americans already had plenty to think about as Toyota's success was continuing apace. With the 60 Series SUV on the market, attention focused again on the 40 Series, now more than 20 years old. The engineers knew that it badly needed replacement but they were also far-sighted enough to see how the 4x4 market was splitting into two, vehicles targeted at working environments, or SUVs likely to be favoured by the general public.

Accordingly the 70 Series, launched in 1984, was designed to serve those who needed a workhorse. Built around a ladder frame with leaf springs and available in a range of body styles, it was tough, with little concession to interior adornment or fancy styling. Toyota did produce a slightly less harsh version, coil-sprung and with suspension to suit the roads, and dubbed it the Prado, but the proper SUV effort was saved for the successor to the 60 Series. From now on, Toyota's Land Cruiser line would consist of two very different products aimed at very different markets.

The 80 Series made its debut in 1990 and certainly made rivals sit up and take notice. It was all-new, right from the chassis through the shell, which boasted curves all over giving the vehicle visually pleasing lines. The solid axles had gone, replaced by coil springs. Permanent all-wheel-drive replaced the part-time units used previously, with a manually-lockable differential mounted centrally between the axles. Newest of the initial engine choices was an economical 163hp turbo diesel but the whole range was soon expanded and updated. Inside the new Land Cruiser, refinement abounded with the options list including such niceties as leather trim and even a refrigerator to keep the drinks cool on a day out. Sales proved so great that Toyota claimed that its factory needed to stay open 24 hours a day for six solid months in order to meet the demand.

Left: In this picture the pick-up truck lineage of Toyota's 4Runner is obvious, though this is the second version that replaced the glassfibre hardtop with a full SUV shell.

American buyers were also being wowed by a new kind of Toyota 4x4, the 4Runner. Launched in 1985, it was based on the company's pick-up truck range and initially boasted a removable glassfibre hardtop. There was a basic utility version and an upmarket model with a slightly less harsh interior, both powered by a 2.4-litre (146ci) engine with a five-speed manual gearbox and two-speed transfer case for the four-wheel-drive. A turbocharged version with a 3-litre engine soon followed.

Toyota redesigned its pick-up trucks in 1990 and the 4Runner got the treatment too. The new version offered four- and six-cylinder engines, two- or four-wheel-drive, and a two- or four-door body shell. More importantly it came as a proper compact SUV, the glassfibre top having been dropped, and with a combination of an independent front suspension and coil springs at the back. Americans in particular loved it and customer satisfaction survey organization JD Power named the 4Runner as its best compact SUV in both 1990 and 1991, ahead of all that the home-grown American manufacturers could muster.

While all this competition between the Americans and the Japanese was developing, the European continent had yet to embrace SUV mania. Though a threat from imported Toyotas and Nissans was beginning to emerge, among European motor manufacturers Land Rover effectively had the market to itself as the German makers in particular showed little interest in this arena – in fact they would spend several more years catching up. There had, however, been a couple of exceptions to this rule, both of them rather odd creations.

Below: The Toyota 4Runner sold well in America, winning best compact SUV awards two years in succession.

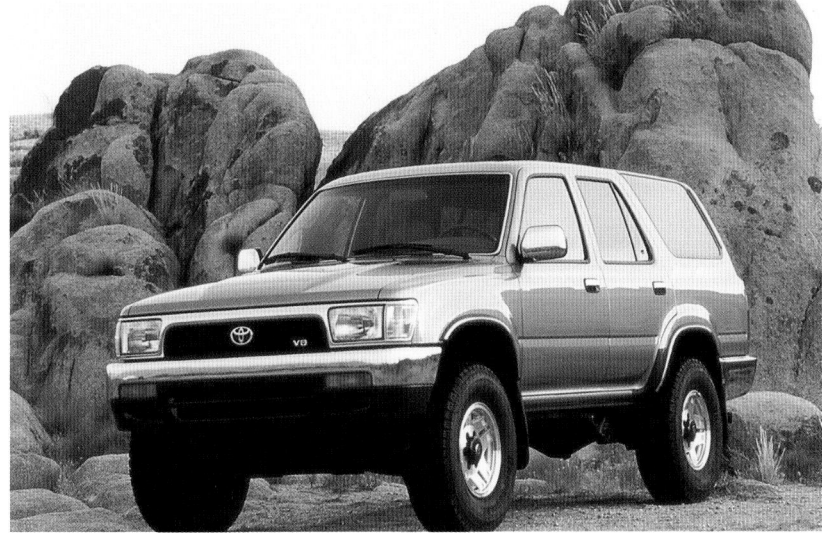

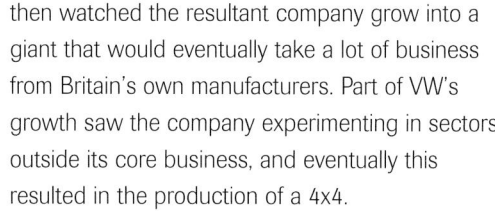

Volkswagen had started life before World War II producing a 'people's car' (Volks-wagen) on the orders of Germany's Nazi Chancellor Adolf Hitler. When hostilities ended, the British occupying forces in Germany rebuilt the VW factory and restarted production of what became the VW Beetle. They

Above and below: A German SUV pioneer? VW's Trekker, or (in the USA) Thing, aimed to take a slice of the growing recreational market in the 1970s.

then watched the resultant company grow into a giant that would eventually take a lot of business from Britain's own manufacturers. Part of VW's growth saw the company experimenting in sectors outside its core business, and eventually this resulted in the production of a 4x4.

In fact the Type 181 was a stop-gap, and a successor to the World War II military Volkswagen, the Kübelwagen. This had effectively been Germany's Jeep – production included 4x4 versions and, for important officers, a fully-enclosed shell. But after the war VW concentrated on its passenger cars and not until the late 1960s did it again dust off the 4x4 file.

At the time a joint project between France, West Germany and Italy was looking at producing a European answer to the Jeep, aiming to design a lightweight amphibious 4x4 mainly for military use. The resultant vehicle was dubbed the Europa-Jeep but the project proceeded very slowly and eventually the scheme petered out with only the Italian Army taking a few hundred vehicles. While awaiting its Europa-Jeeps, the West German army needed to replace its ageing 4x4s, which had been made by German manufacturer DKW since 1956. The military turned to VW, which duly came up with the 181, basically an updated Kübelwagen using

Above: In the 1980s the Range Rover (background) at last gained a European rival in the shape of the G-Wagen from Mercedes-Benz.

components from VW's commercial division. When the Europa-Jeep project finally collapsed, sales of the VW vehicle jumped accordingly, and an updated 183 version ended up being used by many armies across the globe.

VW also found many other sales outlets for the 181/183, both commercially for use in such arenas as forestry and farming, and to private buyers. Having witnessed the rise in popularity of the recreational 4x4, the marketing types in VW's Wolfsburg headquarters believed that people living in warmer climates would quickly see the appeal of its little vehicle, especially if it was given the right name. So in Britain the 183 became the Trekker, while to wow the US market it was dubbed the Thing! Yet the strategy seemed to work, the Thing finding a niche in the growing craze for beach

buggies, and VW sold far more of these vehicles than might have been predicted. Admittedly the Trekker/Thing was a long way from a true SUV, being far more an off-road plaything than a serious everyday vehicle, and VW's management did not pursue this concept. Apart from a brief bout of badge-engineering in the 1990s, the VW badge would not be worn by an SUV until after the turn of the century.

The other European oddity was produced by none other than Mercedes-Benz, which by the 1970s had become renowned across the world as a builder of upmarket sports and saloon cars. The Geländewagen, German for 'off-road vehicle' and soon shortened to G-Wagen, grew out of the failed Europa-Jeep project, with which Mercedes had been involved.

Above: From the start the Mercedes G-Wagen was offered with four different engine options and five different body styles, including this four-door station wagon.

Right: The G-Wagen proved a major success for Mercedes-Benz, so much so that while a new Mercedes GL SUV was launched in 2006, the G-Wagen nevertheless remained in production.

Mercedes' parent company Daimler-Benz already had a strong off-road tradition through its very capable Unimog, a vehicle designed purely to work in the most challenging environments. Knowing that interest in a 4x4 vehicle was still high among the military, and also paying close attention to the growth of the SUV, Daimler-Benz joined forces with Austrian specialist Steyr Puch and the

result was the G 460, unveiled in 1979. This was initially made in five body versions including a two-door station wagon on a 93-inch (2362mm) wheelbase and a four-door version with a 112-inch (2845mm) wheelbase. At launch there were two petrol and two diesel engine choices, ranging from 72hp to 150hp, but this complement was soon expanded. What was lacking was permanent four-

Left: The mid-1980s saw Range Rover tackling its ever-growing number of competitors with the Vogue, a range-topping model with a long list of extras included, such as electric windows and a digital stereo.

wheel-drive – this would not appear until the second-generation version in 1990.

The G-Wagen was, however, extremely capable, and soon a cult grew up around it. Nowhere was this more true than in America, where the G-Wagen's desirability was fuelled by the fact that Mercedes believed there was no Stateside market for its tough SUV. The only way Americans could get hold of a G-Wagen was to buy one from a small importer, Europa International in New Mexico, and many did so, undaunted by paying well above Mercedes prices for their vehicle. Incredibly this situation would continue until 2001, four years after Mercedes unveiled its first true lifestyle-orientated SUV, the ML. But that car lies some way ahead in our story.

Many observers considered the launch of the Mercedes G-Wagen to be a direct response to the Range Rover. The upmarket British SUV was selling extremely well across much of the globe – by 1975 two-thirds of all Range Rovers built were being exported. They were not going to the United States however – ever more stringent regulations particularly concerning emissions dissuaded Land Rover from committing its showpiece product to a US adventure.

Sales were kept high by constant development – the official four-door version of 1981 was followed by major transmission changes in 1983. The fitting of a five-speed manual gearbox made long-distance motorway cruising all the more comfortable, but Range Rover fans were less sure about the fully-automatic gearbox which joined the options list, suspecting that one needed the direct control of a manual gearbox when tackling the toughest off-road conditions. But such fears proved unfounded – the new auto unit worked in perfect harmony with the high and low-range transfer gearboxes, leaving the driver free to concentrate on steering. There were constant styling upgrades too, culminating in a range-topping 'Vogue' version which came with lots of desirable extras such as electric windows, heated remote control mirrors, headlight washers and a digital stereo system – common equipment in today's cars, nirvana to the European SUV buyer of the mid-1980s.

Americans finally received their first Range Rovers in 1987, and at the same time the range was extended by the first diesel version. Finding the right diesel proved a problem, an Italian specialist, Stabilimenti MeccaniciVM SpA, was eventually chosen to produce a four-cylinder 2.4-litre (146ci) unit with 113hp. Where it really scored was on fuel economy – official figures quoted 25.6mpg (11lit/100km) compared to the 15.4 (18.3lit/100km) of the smaller of the two V8 petrol options.

1979 Mercedes G-Wagen 280
Engine:
In-line 6-cyl petrol
Capacity:
2746cc (167.5ci)
Power:
156hp
Transmission:
4-speed manual, selectable 4WD
Construction:
Body-on-frame
Suspension:
Trailing arms, solid axles, coil springs
Brakes:
Front disc, rear drum
Weight:
4553lb (2065kg)
Top speed:
98mph (158kph)
0-62mph (100kph):
14.6 seconds

Above and below: Extended wheelbases and upmarket 'County' styling distinguished Land Rover's signature line in the late 1980s.

Meanwhile the Land Rover line was feeling the benefits of the Range Rover success story. The County had effectively filled the gap between the workhorse Land Rovers and their upmarket SUV sister, but just a year later the 109-inch (2769mm) Land Rover made way for the new 110, and 12 months after that the 89 became the 90. Soon

renamed 'One-Ten' and 'Ninety', both represented evolution from their predecessors, looking every inch traditional Land Rovers encased in new, more aerodynamic shells. 'We operate in a conservative market that appreciates evolution rather than revolution,' said Land Rover Managing Director Tony Gilroy. Under the skin they had lost none of their all-round ability, but they made use of all the techniques that had been learnt in developing the Range Rover – and they reflected the changing DNA of the SUV. There was coil spring suspension for example, which made for a far more comfortable ride. Four-cylinder engines were matched to five-speed gearboxes, again for improved road manners, while interiors were upgraded. For the first time some families considered buying a Land Rover instead of a typical estate car and Land Rover noticed – the first set of upgrades to the 110 saw the sliding side windows replaced by versions with winders while County models gained an item that was formerly anathema to the Land Rover – carpets.

Voyage of Discovery

In 1989 this progression led Land Rover to carry out a root and branch reform in much the way Toyota had eight years earlier, separating its traditional business, that of the workhorse, from the growing SUV market. The Ninety and One-Ten were relaunched as the Defender and refocused to satisfy Land Rover's core market with much of the distinctive SUV trappings stripped out. For the SUV buyer, and to counter the growing influence of Japanese imports, an all-new line was created. Unveiled at the Geneva Motor Show in March, the Discovery looked like no previous Land Rover – but it did look rather like the Range Rover. Underneath the gloss, however, sat the proven, tough mechanical hardware of the Defender on a Range Rover chassis. But there was new technology too – permanent four-wheel-drive was a given, while debuting on the Discovery was a clever new device called Hill Descent Control. This system, still a feature of today's Land Rovers, allowed drivers to descend a

steep slope without touching the brakes, electronics keeping everything in control and the vehicle pointing in the right direction. The Discovery took a while to become accepted in the marketplace, but soon sales were soaring – yet again Land Rover had moved the market on and maintained its position at the top of the European SUV chart.

Above: Land Rover's rethink of 1989 saw the Ninety and One-Ten relaunched as the Defender. A new model, the Discovery (below), appeared to plug the gap between the Defender and Range Rover.

Above: The well-appointed interior of the Discovery was almost up to Range Rover standards.

Right: Sales of the Discovery were slow at first but then quickly gained ground with appreciative customers.

Below: The distinct step in the roof line of the Discovery helped to distinguish it from the then slightly smaller Range Rover.

In truth at this time little in Europe could challenge Land Rover, but the continent had already made a seminal contribution to the SUV story – yet one whose effects would be for many years confined to the USA. The company concerned was Renault. The French manufacturer was desperate for a foothold in the potentially lucrative American market, something the management thought could be achieved by taking a stake in Jeep owner AMC. So in 1979 Renault bought almost half of the American company, taking a controlling interest and immediately initiating a major research programme aimed at establishing exactly where the SUV market was heading. The findings suggested that compact SUVs, aimed directly at the private buyer and not simply converted from military or commercial vehicles, were definitely the way to go. Armed with these conclusions, Renault donated £140 million ($250 million) of funding and some of its best designers to the AMC division, all focused on creating what would become one of the defining models of the SUV timeline – the Jeep Cherokee.

In late 1983 the US media gathered at Borrego Springs, California for its first look at the Cherokee line, and initial shock soon turned to adoration. This vehicle was so different from what had gone before, right down to its foundations – the ladder chassis and bolted-on body had made way for a monocoque unibody construction, in either two- or four-door format. This feature immediately gave the Cherokee a major ride comfort advantage on the road – where SUVs were now tending to spend more of their working lives. Chevrolet made the most of this with a wide range of styling and trim options, both inside and out, while more significantly, buyers could choose from part-time or permanent four-wheel-drive systems, matching the Cherokee to their requirements. Power was supplied by a choice of two petrol engines, with a 2.5-litre (152ci) four

cylinder or a 2.8-litre (170ci) V6 that was actually supplied by rival Chevrolet. The Wagoneer name survived too, applied to what was now essentially a styling version of the new Cherokee and which was distinguished by such niceties as side panels in a wood-grain finish.

Rave reviews came thick and fast, the Cherokee clocking up a clutch of best 4x4 awards among the media. Quite simply it was so far ahead of its time that it was able to soldier on in the same basic form, with only detail improvements, for the best part of a decade. The biggest changes were to the engines. From 1985 a four-cylinder turbo diesel was offered, the 2.1-litre (128ci) unit producing 85hp and sourced from Renault. Two years later in 1987 AMC dropped the 2.8-litre Chevrolet petrol engine in favour of its own 4-litre (244ci) in-line six-cylinder unit.

Below: Jeep still aimed to appeal to upmarket buyers, with the Cherokee Wagoneer retaining its distinguishing two-tone wood-style trim.

Above and below right: The Cherokee racked up a clutch of best SUV awards and stayed in production with only minor changes for more than 10 years.

1993 Jeep Cherokee 4.0 Limited

Engine:

In-line 6-cyl petrol

Capacity:

3960cc (241.5ci)

Power:

184hp

Transmission:

4-speed auto, permanent 4WD

Construction:

Unitary

Suspension:

Solid axles, front coil spring, rear leaf spring

Brakes:

Front disc, rear drum

Weight:

3283lb (1489kg)

Top speed:

112mph (180kph)

0-60mph (97kph):

9.5 seconds

From here on the Cherokee/Wagoneer became very much AMC's SUV standard-bearer although its other Jeep models remained in production, including the Grand Wagoneer station wagon which retained the old-style body shell and V8 powerplant and survived until 1991. Production of the most traditional Jeep, the CJ-7, was ended in 1986, just a year after the last versions of its predecessor, the CJ-5, were made. In their place came a new model built using much of the Cherokee's mechanical hardware and called the Wrangler. This vehicle suited the needs of the traditional off-roading fan, while the Cherokee served the ever growing urban SUV market and was bought by families who used it as their main vehicle. As an aside, AMC was also producing a four-wheel-drive car-based station

wagon called the Eagle, using Jeep hardware under an ageing body shell. Some have called this the first sport-utility wagon, as it pre-dated Subaru's four-wheel-drive estate cars by more than 15 years.

With two successful Jeep lines the future should have looked good for AMC, but the Cherokees and Wranglers were propping up a car division that was increasingly unable to compete with Detroit's big three, GM, Ford and Chrysler. Apart from a couple of Renault-sourced vehicles, AMC's car designs dated from the early 1970s and the company had no resources to develop new ones, so it was little surprise when AMC was taken over by the one member of the big three that did not own its own major recreational vehicle line – Chrysler. The deal was done in August 1987 and within months the only part of AMC that remained was Jeep, now accommodated in a new Chrysler division also planning to sell upmarket cars called Eagles. The big loser seemed to be Renault, financier to the Cherokee. For a couple of years the French manufacturer continued to market Jeeps, but it would not play a further part in the SUV story until more than ten years later – and even then only by taking over Japanese manufacturer Nissan. In late 2005 Renault's model line-up still included no SUVs.

The arrival of the Jeep Cherokee/Wagoneer came as a big shock to GM and Ford, both of whom had been successfully breaking into Jeep's market. Having marketed the larger truck-based Chevrolet Blazer and GMC Jimmy for ten years, GM gained a new SUV line in 1982 with two models designated the Chevrolet S10-Blazer and GMC S15-Jimmy, the numbers distinguishing them from the larger models. These were simply rebadged Suzuki SJ models, the first result of a deal forged between the two manufacturers and which gave the Japanese a much-desired foothold in the United States, neatly side-stepping the restrictive import quotas. The agreement was soon strengthened and building began on a joint GM/Suzuki production plant in Canada.

Launched in late 1982 at prices starting from around £5600 ($10,000), the new Blazer and Jimmy were basically two-door 4x4 SUVs made to seat four, though they were also sold in two-wheel-drive form and as pick-up trucks. Three trim levels were on offer, while power options comprised a four-cylinder 2-litre (122ci) offering 83hp (Californians got a 1.9 [116ci] with 82hp built by Japanese maker Isuzu), or a rather more popular 2.8-litre (170ci) V6 with 110 horses – the same engine initially supplied to arch-rival Jeep for the new Cherokee. The only means of distinguishing the Chevrolet version from the GMC model were slight differences to the front and rear styling. The newcomers proved big hits and by 1985 Chevrolet advertising was claiming that the S10 Blazer was 'America's best-selling sport utility vehicle'. Not all the news was good, however. The Suzuki Samurai, effectively a version of the SJ on which the Blazer had been based, sparked a safety scare in the US with stories suggesting it was prone to rolling over.

The third-generation 'full-size' Bronco had been launched by Ford in 1980. This was a defining model for the blue oval, proving so successful that it would last until 1996. It looked the part, with clean lines that appeared to have been created for the vehicle rather than modified from the truck line even though the Bronco was still based on the F-series truck. The 4.9-litre (300ci) straight-six engine

offered at launch was designed to appeal to a now supposedly fuel-conscious America, but the marketing men covered all the bases by ensuring that 5-litre (302ci) and 5.8-litre (351ci) V8s were also available. Soon Ford was jumping on the power train – by 1984 the Bronco's larger V8 was putting out 210hp compared to the 156 of its predecessor and soon the 302 engine's power was climbing too, aided by Ford's engineers who followed arch-rival Chevrolet and fitted their motors with fuel injection.

Meanwhile to keep the Bronco looking fresh, Ford went for a body restyle. The Bronco of 1987 reflected the new trend for more aerodynamic, less brick-like body shapes. In 1991 the Bronco name celebrated its 25th birthday and Ford marked the event with a special Silver Anniversary version – in red. Admittedly it was an exclusive shade called Currant Red, while inside saw the first use of leather upholstery in a Bronco. While planning another body restyle for 1992, Ford chiefs knew that the Bronco story was coming to an end. In the design office were the first sketches for its replacement, the Expedition, a sister model to Ford's just-launched all-new SUV. This was the Explorer, and it would go on to become Ford's most successful SUV. But it would also follow Suzuki's Samurai in generating controversial headlines...

Above: The third-generation Bronco was a major step forward but it was still based around a redesigned truck.

4 Safety Issues as Sales Soar

By the last years of the 1980s the Sports-Utility Vehicle occupied a sector of the automotive market that – while well-established – was still growing rapidly. More buyers were being turned on to the appeal of large vehicles whose dominant presence on the highway appeared to offer protection to their occupants, giving them a valuable feeling of security. However, this expansion was about to face its first serious test.

A number of controversies have surrounded the SUV in recent years and the sector is currently under sustained attack – on both sides of the Atlantic but particularly in Britain – over its environmental credentials. But in 1988 the first serious SUV controversy concerned not whether such vehicles were environmentally friendly, but whether they were as safe as buyers believed.

Centrepiece of a major argument that erupted that year was Suzuki's Samurai, the latest version of the SJ and one of the smallest SUVs then on sale in the US market. An American lobby group, the Consumers Union, joined forces with the Center for Auto Safety and the Safety First Coalition to highlight apparently serious concerns over how easily the Samurai could roll over in an accident. Opponents of the Samurai argued that it was being marketed as a fun highway cruiser rather than an

Below and below right: Suzuki's small SUV line had come to global attention with the SJ, pictured here in a typical off-road environment.

off-road vehicle. Suzuki's advertising showed owners commuting to work in Samurais, but its short wheelbase, high centre of gravity and stiff suspension made it a tricky vehicle to control at speed. The Consumers Union magazine *Consumer Reports* highlighted what it dubbed as the Samurai's tendency to roll over and in a test branded the vehicle with a sales-killing 'not acceptable' rating. The Consumers Union followed this with a petition to the US National Highway Traffic Safety Administration (NHTSA) in a bid to have the Samurai recalled as unsafe. After studying the little Suzuki in 1988 the NHTSA officially rejected the request, but it did agree to establish a rollover safety standard for cars and light trucks – in US highway terms the Samurai was classified as the latter.

Suzuki slammed the *Consumer Reports* test, dubbing it biased, but the damage had been done

as Samurai sales plummeted – in America the model that had been selling 10,000-plus a month in 1987 at times dropped below 2000 a year later. Suzuki responded by launching a new small 4x4, dubbed the Vitara in Europe and the Sidekick in America, and also sold by GMC and Chevrolet under various names including the Geo Tracker. It was slightly larger than the Samurai, with a four-inch (102mm) wider track and weighing in some 200lb (91kg) heavier, which helped its stability. It also boasted independent front suspension, while at the back the leaf springs of the Samurai made way for coil versions, all of which aided the road performance. While the consumer groups were still not convinced, most saw the new model as a big improvement on the Samurai. Not only that, the Vitara/Sidekick soon

gained fashion credibility, and it became the vehicle to be seen in on both sides of the Atlantic. Sales rocketed accordingly and Suzuki began meeting the demand with more versions and more engine choices. A 1998cc (122ci) 136hp V6 joined the line-up at the end of 1994 and within two years it jumped to 2495cc (152ci) and 160 horsepower.

Below left: The new Vitara was offered in both two-door and four-door (below) versions.

Above: Isuzu's Trooper was another Japanese SUV to fall foul of concerns expressed by American consumer groups over safety standards.

Trooper wars

By 1995, however, the Consumers Union was locking horns with the SUV sector again. This time the vehicle in the dock was another Japanese import, the Trooper made by Isuzu, and the ensuing battle between the Union and Isuzu became very public. In 1996 *Consumer Reports* tested the Trooper and its General Motors sister vehicle, the Acura SLX, and reported that both tipped up on two wheels during an emergency avoidance manoeuvre. The magazine again branded such performance as 'not acceptable.' Isuzu responded by suing the Consumers Union for libel and 'product disparagement', claiming £135 million ($242 million) in damages. In 2000 a jury in a federal court decided that the Union had not intentionally set out to damage the Trooper's reputation and therefore was not liable for damages, though the jury added that one comment in the *Consumer Reports* piece,

stating that Isuzu should never have allowed the Trooper onto the road, had been made 'with a reckless disregard for the truth'. But again the damage had been done to the vehicle, and Isuzu watched US sales of the Trooper slide.

That year the NHTSA announced a new system for measuring rollover risks in vehicles, but the Consumers Union argued that the rating was inadequate as the tests were not carried out on moving vehicles. Within a year *Consumer Reports* was stamping its 'not acceptable' brand on another SUV, this time contending that Mitsubishi's Montero had tipped onto two wheels while making sharp turns at 37mph (60kph) – not surprisingly Mitsubishi disputed the test. And the problems were not confined to SUVs – in Europe Mercedes-Benz was forced to recall its new A-Class mini people-carrier after a Scandinavian magazine turned one over while making a 'moose avoidance test'.

The next big safety scare involved not rollovers but tyres, and pitched two of America's giants against one another. The vehicle concerned was Ford's Explorer, which launched in 1991 and quickly became America's best-selling SUV. But in August 2000 trouble erupted when Ford started recalling 6.5 million Firestone tyres mainly fitted to Explorers. Allegations surfaced of treads peeling from the tyres during high speed driving or in hot conditions, leading to 1400 accidents and 174 deaths. In the ensuing fall-out the head of Bridgestone, Firestone's owner, resigned and Ford and Firestone ended a relationship that had lasted more than a century. By 2001, however, Firestone was fighting back against the claims, arguing that tests done on its behalf by Ohio State University had shown that the Explorer was harder to control than other SUVs after a tyre blow-out. Firestone claimed that Ford was blaming the tyres to cover up problems with its SUV and asked the US government to investigate the vehicle, but Ford responded in determined fashion, stating that its 'real-world' data showed the Explorer to be one of the safest vehicles on the road.

The NHTSA duly studied the Explorer and in 2002 rejected Firestone's claim. 'The data does not support Firestone's contention that Explorers stand out from other SUVs with respect to its handling characteristics following a tread separation,' said NHTSA Administrator Jeffrey Runge. *Car & Driver* magazine had also tested the Explorer's stability and failed to tip one over – it concluded that this was due to its test driver staying calm, arguing that many of the rollovers were probably caused by less experienced drivers panicking and over-reacting when the tyre failed. By now Ford had replaced more than 13 million Explorer tyres, the problem had been linked to 271 accident deaths and both companies were reeling under hundreds of personal injury lawsuits, some of which are outstanding to this day.

Such high-profile scares came amid a growing concern over SUVs' place in the automotive world. Other accusations levelled against the vehicles included the poor carrying ability of some 4x4s, meaning they could easily be overloaded, and the dangers to occupants of cars hit in an accident by a

Below: Ford knew it had a winner in its Explorer of 1991, but what the designers did not expect was that it became involved in the biggest SUV safety controversy yet.

larger, heavier SUV – particularly if the impact was in the car's side. Yet despite all this negative publicity SUV sales continued to soar – in 2000 some 2.8 million were sold to US drivers, which equated to 17 per cent of the market, more than four per cent up on 1999 and this in the year that the Explorer crisis had erupted.

Part of the reason for this growth was that manufacturers, particularly in America, concentrated on giving consumers just what they wanted, and the range of available SUVs had never been wider. The days of SUVs being created from full-time off-road working vehicles had gone – now from the very first sketches on the designer's drawing board they were being designed and built with the highway in mind, aiming to fulfil the needs of consumers who wanted big, tough-looking vehicles but ones equipped with all the comforts too.

The Explorer was clear evidence of this thinking. Replacing the Bronco in 1991, it topped the sales charts from the moment it hit showrooms – in fact many observers credit the Explorer with transforming the SUV sector from a niche to a mainstream market. It was in some ways an old-style SUV in that it had a pick-up truck sister, the Ford Ranger, but it was also highly luxurious, with

four trim levels. These were topped by the Eddie Bauer, an elite version named in association with an outdoor clothing and sporting goods chain and boasting such desirables as two-tone paintwork and alloy wheels. From the start Ford tried to establish two identities for its newcomer – the two-door sat on a 102-inch (2597mm) wheelbase and was aimed at sportier types looking for manoeuvrability, while the four-door was designed as family transport, its 112-inch (2844mm) wheelbase freeing up extra interior space. You could buy your Explorer with two- or four-wheel-drive (the latter including a low-range transfer 'box for proper off-road ability), while initially a four-speed auto transmission was combined with the only engine choice, a 4-litre (243ci) V6 petrol unit offering 155hp. Within a year a five-speed manual gearbox joined the range, and a new Limited version of the four-door was launched. This was even better equipped than the Eddie Bauer, boasting extra styling and a centre console with built-in compass and thermometer. Japanese manufacturer Mazda, in which Ford now had a large stake, also offered a two-door Explorer clone, initially 4WD only and dubbed the Navajo – only its grille, rear lights and wheels differed from the Explorer.

2000 Ford Explorer
4.0 Sport
Engine:
V6 petrol
Capacity:
4011cc (244.7ci)
Power:
205hp
Transmission:
5-speed auto, automatic
4WD
Construction:
Body-on-frame
Suspension:
Torsion bars, rear leaf
springs
Brakes:
Discs all round
Weight:
3975lb (1803kg)
Top speed:
115mph (185kph)
0-60mph (97kph):
8.4 seconds

In 1995 Ford took the opportunity to give the Explorer a sales boost with a makeover that simply improved a package that many Americans already coveted. The Mk2 version boasted major changes, the most significant being to the suspension where the truck-derived twin traction beam unit made way for an independent unit giving the SUV road manners that were far more car-like. Both the exterior and interior were restyled, the outside now boasting a more aerodynamically-friendly sloping nose and new bumpers front and rear, which added four inches (102mm) to the vehicle's length. Ford separated the four-door and two-door models into Explorer and Explorer Sport ranges while a new trim level joined the line-up, the Expedition brand effectively replacing Eddie Bauer. The V6 engine remained though by 1996 it had been joined by a 5-litre (305ci) offering 210hp. But no diesel was offered and that never has been an Explorer option. The Mk2 had already gained an improved four-wheel-drive unit – called 'Control Trac' it automatically applied power to the front wheels when slippery conditions demanded. Previously the driver had been required to make the decision and manually select AWD. By 1997, however, the options list for top-end Explorers included permanent four-wheel-drive.

Below: In 1997 Ford released an upmarket cousin to the Explorer under its Mercury brand – the Mountaineer.

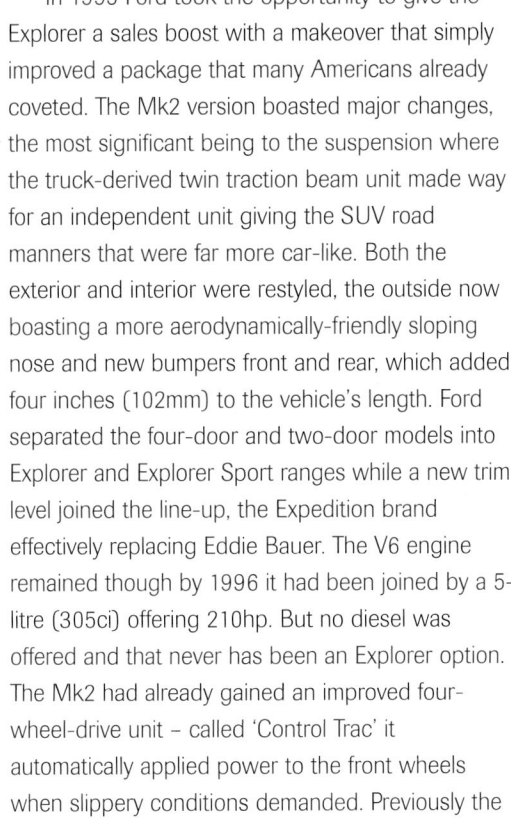

Above: Ford's first European compact SUV was the Maverick, which was little more than a rebadged Nissan Terrano II and which was outsold by the Japanese manufacturer's version.

Exploring Europe

While a big success at home, the Explorer fared less well abroad. It was available in Europe from 1997 but made little impression there. For the European markets Ford came up with a smaller model, the Maverick – European audiences were of course blissfully unaware of the highly successful Maverick coupé car of the 1970s as it had been a US market model only. Again the Maverick SUV was an example of Ford working with a Japanese manufacturer, but not Mazda this time. The first Maverick 4x4 had been sold in Australia and was basically a rebadged Nissan Patrol, but for its launch in Europe Ford chose to make use of a rather newer Nissan SUV, the Terrano II.

Nissan's first Terrano had launched in 1986, though to US buyers it was better known as the Pathfinder. Based on a pick-up truck, it was a chunky 4x4, two-door only and aimed squarely at the leisure SUV market. In 1993 Nissan came up with the Terrano II, basically an all-new model and created by the Japanese company's UK design office. It still relied on a ladder frame with either a two- or four-door shell mounted on it, with part-time four-wheel-drive and was powered by either a 2389cc (146ci) petrol engine of 124hp or a turbo-diesel offering 99 horses from its 2664cc (163ci).

A front suspension combining double wishbones with torsion bars aided the road manners, and Ford dubbed its Maverick version – nothing more than the Nissan with more equipment – 'the best SUV in the world'. But such claims held little water in image-conscious Europe where buyers were still not convinced by a Ford SUV and tended to buy Nissans in preference – already Japan's motor industry was building a reputation for reliability.

Ford was not the only manufacturer trying to spread its SUV message to the European market. Chrysler Jeep was in expansion mode too, readying itself for a launch into Britain, and more importantly taking on the Ford Explorer, by producing an all-new and bigger version of the Cherokee. First shown at the 1989 Detroit Auto Show as 'Concept 1', the Grand Cherokee launched onto the US market in 1992, Jeep's first all-new vehicle for a decade. Britons would not see it until 1997 and then only in left-hand-drive form. As its name suggested the Grand Cherokee was a big sister to the still mass-selling Cherokee, and was a full-size four-door SUV on a 105.9-inch (2690mm) wheelbase, four inches (102mm) longer than the Cherokee. It was of monocoque rather than ladder-frame construction, which added to its road manners, but it lacked none of the off-road ability one expected from a Jeep.

Indicative of this was the Quadra-coil suspension, which, rather than a fully independent set-up, combined coil springs with the solid axles of a true off-roader.

Power came from a 4-litre (243ci) in-line six with 190hp on tap, and customers could choose from three trim levels – standard equipment included anti-lock brakes on all four wheels and a driver's airbag, both newcomers to the SUV sector. Within a year a 5.2-litre (317ci) V8 with 220 horses joined the range in an upmarket model dubbed the Grand Wagoneer. It retained the woodgrain side panel effect seen on earlier Wagoneer models. The bigger motor gave the Grand Cherokee a power advantage over its rivals from Ford, Chevrolet and Toyota, and made it a big hit with anyone who needed to tow a

trailer on a regular basis, horse owners for example. As for transmission options, the Jeep owner could choose Command-Trac, which was an automatic part-time system, Selec-Trac which allowed manual selection of 4WD (this meaning that it could be used at all times and not just on slippery surfaces), and Quadra-Trac, a full-time 4WD system.

Jeep's smaller SUV was not forgotten and in 1995 the US maker struck a blow against European rivals such as Land Rover when it offered diesel engines in the Cherokee. Diesel power had found (and still does find) popularity in Europe where petrol is significantly more expensive than it is in the USA. There was a five-strong model range all powered by a 2499cc (152ci) four-cylinder turbodiesel producing 116bhp.

Above: Ten years after the launch of the Cherokee, Jeep produced a larger sister vehicle, the Grand Cherokee.

Above: The Grand Cherokee's interior was designed to satisfy the more exacting requirements of the demanding SUV buyer.

Left: The Chevrolet Suburban name was a remarkable survivor from pre-war motoring. By the late 1990s it was applied to this very large SUV.

Over at General Motors much was also occurring. During the decade the Chevrolet S10 Blazer and GMC S15 Jimmy had spawned a host of derivatives, topped by such upmarket trendy models as the GMC Typhoon and Oldsmobile Bravada. 1995 brought new versions, still closely Suzuki-related. There were still two- and four-door versions, but they were distinctly different with the smaller vehicle boasting a bold forward-sloping C-pillar. The shells as a whole were smoother, the advantage of which was both aerodynamic and visual. Both versions measured up almost 5 inches (127mm) longer and 2.5 inches (63.5mm) wider. There was just one power option, a 4.3-litre (262ci) V6 carried over from the previous model but reduced by five horsepower to 195hp. Two- or four-wheel-drive was offered, which was controlled by a four-speed auto transmission and matched to a wide range of suspensions dependent on what you wanted your Blazer/Jimmy to do.

Above: Chevrolet's Blazer/Jimmy line spawned new models in 1995, with smoother body shells matched to mechanical changes.

Right: The two- and four-door versions of the Blazer, the latter seen here, boasted distinctly different looks.

Before long the S10 designation had disappeared as General Motors finally solved its identity crisis by ending its practice of manufacturing two differently-sized SUV lines both called the Blazer and Jimmy. The original full-sized versions had been selling alongside their younger siblings for years, each season ushering in subtle improvements. 1992, however, saw the launch of a new version and the Jimmy had its name changed to the GMC Yukon. Within two years the Blazer had been rebadged as the Chevrolet Tahoe.

The Tahoe/Yukon were closely related to another GM model which had been steadily updated through the decades. This was the Suburban, one of the earliest names to appear in our story and one which was still selling, basically on its go-anywhere ability and huge interior space – three rows of occupants could be happily accommodated. In the same year that the new Tahoe/Yukon models appeared, Chevrolet gave the Suburban a serious

makeover, the model adopting the much smoother styling that had been applied four years earlier to the pick-up trucks on which it was based. While now seen by many as an SUV, it was still basically a station wagon version of the pick-ups, built around a ladder chassis. Its priority was to get people from A to B rather than giving them a pleasant ride along the way. But the 1992 versions did offer some concessions to comfort – independent front suspension for example. Two- and four-wheel-drive versions were available with engines ranging from 5.0 to 7.0 litres (305 to 426ci). Basically it was big,

Above: The Jimmy was a long-lasting name in the GMC line-up...

Below: ...as was the Blazer in sister-company Chevrolet's model range.

Above: As can be seen in this 1996 publicity shot, Chevrolet still promoted its Blazer as a vehicle that was happy in an off-road environment.

and it liked its fuel, petrol only of course – and so it has remained to this day, spawning a GMC version, the Yukon XL, and eventually a Cadillac model, the Escalade ESV.

The Yukon and Cadillac gained extra letters after their names to distinguish them from the models that succeeded the Blazer/Jimmy. This was because, having come up with new names for its larger SUVs, GM muddied the waters by also applying the same GMC title to the smaller version. The new GMC Yukon, soon joined by the Chevrolet Tahoe, was built around a shortened version of the Suburban's

platform – a move which some might see as backward when many rivals were dumping truck chassis for the monocoques which offered much better road manners. The range included two- and four-door versions, while the single engine choice was the same 5.7-litre (348ci) V8 that powered the Suburban. A year later a 6.5-litre (396ci) diesel was added, but only to the four-wheel-drive two-door Yukon variant. A smaller engine would not appear until the second-generation Tahoe/Yukon of 2000 – models that would also spawn a third brand in the Cadillac Escalade.

Right: Effectively replacing the Blazer and Jimmy names in the late 1990s were the Chevrolet Tahoe, seen here, and the GMC Yukon.

As these changes were taking place, a large slice of the market was still being swallowed up by Japanese imports. As we have seen, the two versions of the Toyota Land Cruiser, and the newer 4Runner, found many owners across the globe. In 1995 a third Land Cruiser, the 90 Series 'Prado', joined the line-up. It had evolved from the 70 Series, using the 4Runner's chassis and was designed as a workhorse in similar fashion to Land Rover's Defender. Far more relevant to our story, however, was the new Toyota that was now on sale. A small and very stylish SUV unveiled at the 1993 Tokyo Motor Show, it was called the RAV4, and its name revealed the exact thinking behind its construction – the acronym stood for 'Recreational Active Vehicle, four-wheel-drive' and this is exactly what this was. In the RAV4 the SUV finally abandoned its off-road

roots to become a fashion item – this was the SUV that you would most likely see in the supermarket car park, outside school at home time and, notably, many of the RAV4's buyers were women.

The first two-door versions offered permanent four-wheel-drive, controlled by a five-speed manual or four-speed auto gearbox and powered by a 1998cc (122ci) four-cylinder petrol engine of 129hp. Sales figures soon convinced Toyota chiefs that they had a hit on their hands, as did the awards – the model launched into the US in 1996 and took three prizes that year – including 'Best Small SUV' from *Consumer Reports* magazine. Within two years power levels had increased and a four-door version on an extended wheelbase joined the range. No diesel was available though – that would not arrive until 2002.

Above: Toyota's RAV4 of 1993 was an SUV revolution, aimed firmly at leisure buyers.

Above: Toyota gained a serious new home-grown rival when Honda launched the CR-V in 1995. It may have been more soft-roader than off-roader, but customer demand for this stylish SUV was strong.

Rivals watched the RAV4 with interest, and none more so than Toyota's biggest home-market competitor, Honda. A young company – Soichiro Honda had only started making motorcycles in 1948 – Honda had gained a reputation for modern cars, but in the SUV game it was well behind the times, all its 4x4s being rebadged versions of other manufacturers' products built under licence. For example, the Honda Crossroad was actually a version of Land Rover's Discovery, the Passport a reworked Isuzu. That all changed in 1995 with the launch of the CR-V, an all-new in-house SUV. A four-door five-seater originally powered by a 1973cc (120ci) engine of 131hp, it was created along exactly the same lines as the RAV4 and between them the two created a new SUV sub-class, quickly dubbed, in not entirely complimentary fashion, 'Soft-Roaders'. But such descriptions did not worry Honda – CR-V sales proved so strong that before long the company started making them in Britain as well as in Japan.

Meanwhile yet another Japanese manufacturer was steadily gaining its own place in the market – Mitsubishi. Unlike Honda this was a very old name, an engineering firm dating back to the 1870s, but one that had gone through a similar early SUV history to Toyota. Mitsubishi spent much of the 1950s manufacturing Jeeps under franchise, mainly for military use, and would continue to do so right

up until 1999. Eventually Mitsubishi used its knowledge to design its own 4x4, which was unveiled at the 1979 Tokyo Motor Show as the Pajero – the name is Patagonian and is identified with strength and perseverance. The Pajero arrived in the US two years later as the Montero, and was sold in Britain and Japan as the Shogun. Versions ranged from two to four doors, with part-time four-wheel-drive and engines including a 2555cc (156ci) 103hp, a 2972cc (181ci) V6 with 141hp and a unit that claimed the title of first turbo-diesel in an off-roader, this a 2346cc (143ci) offering 84hp. Everything was built onto a ladder frame with independent front suspension but old-style leaf springs at the rear.

Mitsubishi updated the Shogun/Montero in 1991, fitting it with a smoother shell boasting rounded contours and adding a larger version, along with a convertible. By now there were two petrol and two diesel engines ranging up to 208hp, a new 'Super Select' four-wheel-drive unit that offered a range of modes, and a clever chassis that even included shock absorbers adjustable to three separate modes. In the next few years many of these features would find their way onto a wider line-up of SUVs, while Mitsubishi would be among those to embrace the soft-roader concept. Also heading in this direction would be a very surprising name, as will be revealed in the next chapter.

Meanwhile the 1990s saw the launch of one SUV that really bucked the trend – and one which acquired a cult following of its own. The company was the same that had created the Jeep – but its military division, which was separated from the civilian Jeep line and sold off in the 1980s. By 1983 AMC General, as the military division was known, was busy building an all-new, very big and tough transport vehicle for the US Army. It was called the Humvee, then the Hummer, and by 1991 thoughts turned to producing a civilian version. There was a good reason for this – the Hummer was now a TV star, seen on screens around the world (and particularly in America) every night as it led the way in 'Operation Desert Storm', the Gulf War of 1991 to reclaim Kuwait from the invading forces of Iraq. The story goes that when popular movie tough guy Arnold Schwarzenegger had his own version created for the road, demand multiplied enormously.

The vehicle launched in October 1992, and was quite unlike any other SUV on the market. To begin with it was huge, more than seven feet (2.13m)

wide, and heavy, weighing in at 6840lb (3100kg). Even with a diesel engine fuel economy could drop below 10mpg (29lit/100km) in a vehicle that was not exactly fast – an owner would not expect more than 65mph (105kph). With a minimum selling price of £28,000 ($50,000), this was a niche player in the market – much to the relief of the anti-SUV brigade, who were not exactly happy about massive Hummers tearing up their streets. Sales never really took off, but this would not be the end of the Hummer story.

As we have already seen, even companies as big as Ford were by this time not above a degree of badge-engineering. One of the brand names that the blue oval owned was Mercury and 1997 saw the launch onto the US market of the Mountaineer, quite simply an upmarket Ford Explorer brimming with extra equipment and chrome trim and capitalizing on the growing demand for executive SUVs. This move came just in time to respond to a new tide of executive 4x4s from Europe – German manufacturers had finally woken up to the appeal of the SUV.

Below: The anti-SUV? A Gulf War and a Hollywood star helped create a demand for the nothing-short-of-outrageous Hummer.

5 Enter the Executives

During the second half of the 1990s the Sports-Utility Vehicle was a familiar sight across the globe, and the only sector of the worldwide motor industry that continued to record sustained growth, year after year. Yet one major centre of the car business remained seemingly indifferent to the charms of the SUV.

This was Germany, home of much of Europe's motor industry. In particular the German premium manufacturers, Mercedes-Benz, BMW and Audi, appeared to have little interest in making such vehicles. And as far as the executive buyers of the upmarket products manufactured by this trio were concerned, the thought of the prized three-pointed star of Mercedes or the kidney grille of BMW appearing on what was basically an off-roader, well it seemed laughable.

Below: Mercedes-Benz shifted the focus of the SUV sector. Its ML of 1997 ushered in the era of the German-built executive 4x4.

Behind the closed doors of the design studios, however, a very different view was being taken. The German brands were now noticing that, particularly in America, the SUV had rapidly become an executive vehicle. Stateside buyers investing in the latest 4x4s perhaps found off-road ability a useful extra, but they handed over their dollars because the machines looked big, dominant and impressive on the road, and vitally now came fitted with all the 'toys' one expected in an executive car.

Manufacturers were happy to meet such tastes with more heavily-accessorized, upmarket versions of their SUVs, for which of course they could charge more. It was the kind of market that the likes of Mercedes and BMW knew very well; however, such makers had never previously applied their brand values to large, big-wheeled vehicles fitted with four-wheel-drive transmissions.

Mercedes of course already made a 4x4, the G-Wagen, but this vehicle was far more closely allied to the German manufacturer's commercial department, and was much more a tough off-roader than a comfortable runabout. It was also, of course, excluded from what could have potentially been one of its biggest markets, America, unless buyers paid a hefty premium and ordered their G-Wagen from one tiny independent importer.

In marked contrast to this attitude, Japan's auto manufacturers were not only selling their increasingly upmarket SUVs on the North American continent, they were also building them there – though the setting up of Stateside plants was to a great extent a means to an end, neatly getting around restrictive quotas that America imposed on imported vehicles. Mercedes management realized that in order to really make a mark in the USA they would need to follow the Japanese example and set up a factory in the heart of SUV territory. They duly built their plant in Tuscaloosa, Alabama and from 1997 it began turning out the Mercedes ML, indisputably an SUV, but one aimed squarely at the market that the Germans knew so well.

Top and above: The Mercedes ML was an SUV, but an SUV with a level of refinement familiar to buyers of the German manufacturer's cars.

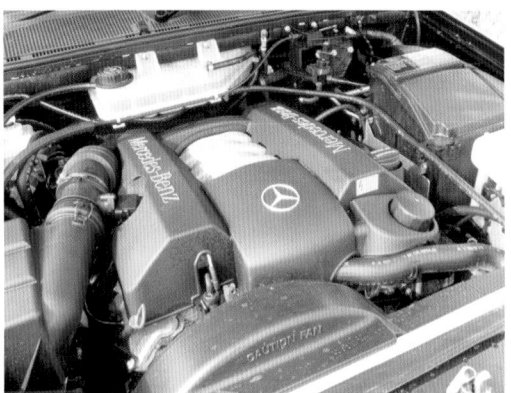

Above: A surprising decision to opt for traditional body-on-frame construction gave the ML road manners that were rather less Mercedes-like than usual.

Right: The ML had plenty of power under the bonnet, with up to 342hp available.

The ML combined what Mercedes knew about executive cars, which was quite a lot, with what it knew about 4x4 SUVs, which was rather less and knowledge acquired mainly through experience with the G-Wagen. The result was, in truth, not the best contender in the market. The ML's styling gave it quite a soft image, whereas rivals tended to go for a bolder, domineering presence. The newcomer did boast the plush interior that Mercedes buyers expected, but this was contained within a shell built in traditional style, bolted on top of a ladder-frame chassis. Of course such construction allowed for reasonable off-road ability, but performance on the blacktop, prime Mercedes customer territory, was to a degree compromised. This was also a time when Mercedes build quality often failed to reach the standard buyers expected from the brand. Yet none of this seemed to matter, as the ML became an overnight hit. It was not short of power – 3.2 and 5-litre (195 and 305ci) engines were soon joined by a 5.4-litre (329ci) AMG sporting version offering an impressive 342hp, along with a duo of diesels. Critics who had scoffed at the combination of the three-pointed star and an SUV were forced to eat their words as buyers went for the newcomer in a big way. In America the ML found plenty of willing customers, while in Europe it created a whole new segment – the premium SUV.

Mercedes appeared to be leading the way, but it was a safe bet that what had become clear to the designers in Stuttgart was equally obvious to the Munich-based team of deadly rival BMW. The market had to wait three years, however, before BMW unveiled its contender in this new sector, the X5. BMW enjoyed one major advantage over Mercedes – it already had a plant up and running in SUV country, in this case Spartanburg, South Carolina, a factory set up in 1994 initially to build the Z3 sports roadster. BMW's marketing department also had a clear idea of the kind of vehicle that was required to take on the Mercedes ML – and the word Utility did not feature anywhere in the product description of a BMW.

The author was one of a party of UK journalists invited out to Spartanburg in 2000 to witness the launch of the X5, and at a lavish ceremony the new vehicle was unveiled and immediately described by our American hosts as 'the world's first SAV, or Sports-Activity Vehicle'. BMW was daring to state what everyone knew – precious few of its new X5s would ever leave the road behind to head off on a forest track or mountain path. Like the Mercedes the BMW offered a fair degree of off-road ability and included such electronic aids as Hill Descent Control, a system that allowed the driver to control the vehicle's speed down a steep gradient without touching the brakes. But the plush leather, climate control, quality hi-fi and satellite navigation, and perhaps more tellingly the unitary body structure with all-round tarmac-friendly independent suspension, indicated exactly who was expected to buy an X5. The price tag was another major indicator, ranging from £22,000 ($39,000) for the 3-litre (183ci) six-cylinder petrol model and around £28,000 ($50,000) for its 4.2-litre (256ci) V8 sister.

Judging by the reaction of the American media, BMW got the X5 just right. Reviewing the newcomer *Autoweek* wrote 'Yes, we were (are) skeptical about a BMW-ute, but the X5 is incredibly good,' while *Road & Track* added to the praise in its April 2000 issue, 'Though not cheap...the Munich-engineered, Spartanburg, South Carolina-built X5 is the most enthusiast-friendly Sport Activity Vehicle yet.'

Challenge from Toyota

So the Germans had begun muscling into territory that US names had previously dominated, but the Mercedes ML and BMW X5 were not the only new challengers the home-grown American manufacturers were now forced to battle against. The Japanese had for some years enjoyed very healthy sales of their SUVs in America alongside rapidly growing markets in Europe – now they too were ready and eager to make their mark in the new premium SUV sector. Not surprisingly leading the challenge from the Far East was Toyota, seeing the opportunity to add a whole new revenue stream to its young upmarket brand, Lexus. The badge had made its US debut back in 1989 with the unveiling of the LS400 and ES250 executive saloons at the Detroit Motor Show, and success had been swift. Buoyed by high media praise for Japanese quality and reliability standards, within three years Lexus was outselling both BMW and Mercedes in the US.

Above: The new executive SUV sector took a major step forward in 2000 with the launch of BMW's X5.

Above and below: The Lexus LX 450 proved a big hit in the United States, despite being basically a plusher Toyota Land Cruiser.

The first Lexus 4x4, the LX 450, was launched in 1996, and was positioned as a luxury sports-utility vehicle. Within two months it was topping its segment, taking over the mantle from Britain's big challenger the Range Rover. But the LX 450 was in fact nothing more than an example of badge-engineering. As described in Chapter 3 Toyota's all-encompassing SUV line, the Land Cruiser, had six years earlier progressed to the 80 Series, and the LX 450 was in fact a 4.4-litre (273ci)-engined 80 Series with lots of luxury touches added to the specification. It boasted a four-speed auto transmission and permanent four-wheel-drive and lasted a whole three years on sale. The reason was simple – in 1998 Toyota replaced the 80 Series Land Cruiser with the 100 Series, the most tarmac-friendly version of the model yet. Independent double wishbone front suspension was a prime feature, though those who intended to use their Land Cruisers in tougher environments could choose a stiff coil setup instead. Desirable additions included the ability to carry up to eight occupants and automatic adjustment of the vehicle's ride height from the cockpit depending on the condition of terrain being tackled, while there was also a new engine option, a 4.7-litre (286ci) V8 unit with 235hp on offer. Not surprisingly a Lexus version soon followed, dubbed the LX 470 and still using the V8 engine, but adding an extra fifth speed allied to the auto transmission.

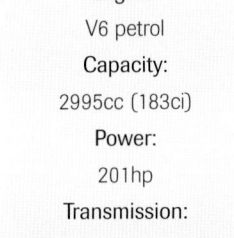

2000 Lexus RX 300
Engine:
V6 petrol
Capacity:
2995cc (183ci)
Power:
201hp
Transmission:
4-speed auto, permanent
4WD
Construction:
Unitary
Suspension:
Independent, wishbones,
coil springs
Brakes:
Discs all round
Weight:
3969lb (1800kg)
Top speed:
112mph (180kph)
0-60mph (97kph):
8.9 seconds

Crossing over the tracks

The same year, however, saw Lexus reveal its answer to the Mercedes ML. The RX 300 was unveiled at the Detroit Auto Show in January, a five-seater intended to sit alongside the bigger and more powerful LX 470. While using mechanicals proven on Toyota models, this was no rebadged Land Cruiser but a new four-door model, with two- or four-wheel-drive options, 2995cc (183ci) 201hp or 3302cc (201ci) 233hp petrol engines and four- or five-speed auto transmissions. While Toyota offered a version called the Harrier observers noted the close resemblance to the Camry saloon and as a result a new motoring phrase was born – the 'Crossover' denoting a vehicle that, while looking like an SUV, was much closer to a muscular car than a proper off-roader. The phrase would soon become regularly used in an SUV market that was beginning to segment into different sectors determined by size, level of refinement and level of off-road prowess.

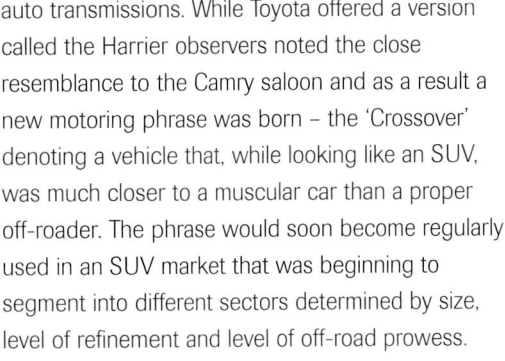

Above left: The LX 450 and its 470 successor established the SUV credentials of Lexus...

Left: ...while the RX 300 became one of the first 'crossover' SUVs.

Above: Toyota's 80 Series Land Cruiser of 1998 was the most road-orientated version yet of the long-running line.

Toyota was not alone in targeting the top end of the SUV market. The Japanese maker's closest rivals, Honda and Nissan, soon set up their own luxury brands, with more than a passing glance at gaining lots of US sales. Honda's executive arm was named Acura. Formed in 1986, it revealed its first SUV a decade later in the Acura SLX. In fact this was a version of the latest Isuzu Trooper, Honda handing the contract to Isuzu as a rapid means of gaining a foothold in America's upmarket SUV sector. The resulting vehicle proved to be an 'old-style' ladder-frame SUV with poor road manners – an untimely defect at the height of the SUV versus *Consumer Reports* magazine court battle over the claimed rollover tendencies of the Trooper. Acura added such niceties as leather trim and a massive sunroof and opened a network of dealers across the States, but the SLX was always a compromise and sales proved very poor. By 1999 it had been

discontinued as Honda realized that to have any hope of real success in the USA it had to follow the example of Lexus.

The SLX replacement, launched two years later in the form of the Acura MDX, was built in Canada. It was immediately branded with the crossover badge as it used much of the mechanical hardware of Honda's Accord passenger car. Just one power option was offered, a 3471cc (212ci) V6 petrol unit with 265hp and a part-time four-wheel-drive system, automatically changing from front-wheel-drive when wheel slippage was detected. While upmarket, the MDX was also practical, with flip-up seats in the cargo area enabling it to carry seven passengers. Emphasizing its executive status, the options list included a DVD entertainment system and satellite navigation. Buyers were impressed as was the media, top magazine *Car & Driver* naming the MDX its 'Best Luxury SUV' in 2001.

To Infiniti and beyond

Nissan's choice for an upmarket name was Infiniti, the brand being established with 51 dealers across America in 1989. The first SUV appeared in 1997. It was named the QX4 and dubbed by industry business newspaper *Automotive News* 'One of Ten Cool Engineering Things'. But yet again this was an example of badge engineering, as the QX4 was little more than a made-over version of Nissan's latest Pathfinder/Terrano. This boasted a unibody construction, the perfect base for creating an executive SUV, though the 160hp offered by the 3.3-litre (200ci) engine was modest compared to rivals, particularly when the Pathfinder's five-speed manual gearbox was replaced by a four-speed auto in the Infiniti variant. The transmission was rather more high-tech, however. Called All-Mode, it could be set for rear-wheel-drive only, automatic all-wheel-drive that distributed power to the front or rear pairs of wheels according to need, and a locked mode that divided torque equally between the front and rear. The QX4 also boasted a low-range gearbox, giving it rather more off-road ability than its direct rivals. Nissan did not stint on the extras either – the QX4's £20,500 ($36,500) base

price included leather seats, wood trim, electric adjustment all over and automatic climate control. Not surprisingly the QX4 was well received, and in 2001 sales were boosted by an update. Notably this addressed the engine deficiencies by replacing the 160hp unit with a 240hp version as well as updating the vehicle's look both inside and out.

Above and below: Nissan aimed to wow affluent Americans with its Infiniti QX4, which came with an impressive options list that included in-car movies.

Right: The new Range Rover of 1994 offered three V8 petrol engine options or a BMW-built diesel.

Opposite above: There was one way in which the new Range Rover differed from its rivals – nothing stopped it! But inside luxury levels were comparable to the best rivals.

Opposite below: Land Rover addressed the Japanese 'soft-roader' challenge with its Freelander of 1997.

Below: It took almost quarter of a century before the original Range Rover made way for this all-new Mk2 in 1994.

Some observers believed that the trend towards premium SUVs had actually started back in 1970 in Britain with the launch of the first Range Rover. Its successor had already been on sale for three years by the time Mercedes kick-started the executive SUV sector. The Range Rover II had been launched in 1994, a long-overdue replacement for the vehicle that had proven so revolutionary back in 1970, though the Mk1 version continued to sell alongside the newcomer for two more years under the 'Range Rover Classic' banner. The Range Rover II was an all-new vehicle but in many ways very similar to its predecessor – it was built on the same length wheelbase, it used the same V8 engine, but now including 4278cc (261ci) 202hp and 4552cc (278ci) 226hp versions. The diesel option was a turbocharged intercooled unit of 2497cc (152ci) offering 136hp and supplied by BMW.

The German maker was now showing a serious interest in Rover and was soon to take the company over. Despite the trend towards ever more tarmac-friendly SUVs the new Range Rover still used beam axle suspension, its designers considering that even the luxury range-topper of the Land Rover line-up had to be capable of coping with the most extreme off-road conditions. But the electronic control aids for the air suspension, using seven different computers, were bang up-to-date compared to its rivals, while other technological innovations included ABS brakes. The new model was longer, wider and taller than its predecessor, with a far smoother, more aerodynamic body, and it boasted specification levels to a degree of luxury that the creators of the 1970 original could not have dreamed of. Yet before long even this was not enough and by 1997 Range Rover was offering limited edition versions that in the UK cost more than £50,000.

Meanwhile Land Rover was also tackling the rise of small sporty SUVs, epitomized by Toyota's RAV4. 1997 saw the launch of the Freelander, an all-new model targeted directly at the leisure market. By Land Rover standards it was revolutionary, particularly as it boasted a unibody construction – heresy to Land Rover traditionalists. The Freelander came in two- or four-door form while a soft-back variant was also offered. Two engines were available, a 1725cc (108ci) four-cylinder petrol unit of 120hp and a diesel V6 of 2497cc (152ci) with 177hp. Yet while the most road-orientated Land Rover yet, the Freelander still conformed to the company's mantra – its specification included a full range of off-road electronic aids, among them Hill Descent Control. When in 1999 the Freelander range was expanded to include a V6 2497cc (152ci) engine of 177hp, sales rocketed, particularly in the US, and the Freelander line has accounted for a great proportion of Land Rover's annual turnover ever since.

Right and below: Ford's answer to the challenge of the Europeans was this, an upmarket Explorer sold as the Mercury Mountaineer.

What, however, of the American manufacturers? How did they react to the mass influx of executive SUVs with their long lists of desirable equipment? The answer was simple – they loaded their own models with extras too. Thus in 1997 Ford made use of its Mercury brand to produce an upmarket cousin to the Explorer. The new model was called the Mercury Mountaineer, and could be supplied in either rear-wheel-drive or permanent four-wheel-drive format. Both were allied to the only engine choice, the 5-litre (305ci) V8 driving through a four-

speed auto transmission. Within a year a V6 motor and five-speed auto gearbox joined the line-up, but of more interest to buyers was the extensive specification list, and the looks that relied heavily on chrome trim outside and wood within. One reviewer reported being told by a dealer that the Mountaineer was attracting many women buyers, because they found it less intimidating than an Explorer yet easy to drive on the road. They also loved its leather interior.

By now Ford had also replaced the full-size Bronco. Establishing a new trend that saw all its SUVs given names beginning with the letter E, 1996 saw the unveiling of the Expedition, a four-door-only model that was certainly a big vehicle – among its targets was Chevrolet's Suburban. While taking six as standard, some versions of the Expedition could seat nine occupants. Still Ford persisted with traditional construction, the Expedition developed directly out of the F-150 pick-up truck. It came in rear- or four-wheel-drive versions, the latter using Ford's Control-Trac system, and the petrol-only engine options initially comprised a 4.6-litre (280ci) V8 of 215hp and a 5.4-litre (330ci) with 230hp. Within two years these were uprated to offer respectively 240 and 260hp. Air suspension could be had, but only as an option, the standard set-up being coils all round.

From the start the Expedition was offered in a range-topping Eddie Bauer variant boasting such niceties as captain's chair front seats trimmed in leather. But to take on the Range Rover seriously,

Left: The Ford Expedition replaced the full-size Bronco as a big brother to the Explorer.

Ford raided its badge box again, this time drawing out Lincoln. The Lincoln Navigator hit the market in 1998, powered by the 5.4-litre (330ci) V8 and boasting leather upholstery, interior trim in walnut, extra soundproofing and rich carpeting underfoot. Second-row passengers got the captain's chairs and a centre console with their own climate control system. The Navigator looked different too, both the front and rear styling were altered to distinguish it from its mainstream sister, and it rode better, the suspension having been softened up compared to the Explorer. Underneath the dressing the Navigator may have been built on a dated chassis compared to its Japanese opposition, but it sold anyway, even at prices of more than £26,000 ($46,000).

Above and left: Ford used the Lincoln badge to create an upmarket Expedition – this is a 1999 Navigator.

Ford also found time to create its own Toyota RAV4/Land Rover Freelander rival. The first Ford Maverick, based on the Nissan Terrano II, had been aimed at Europe but made little impression there. Its replacement was designed to suit a wider audience, and while retaining the Maverick title in Europe, it went on sale at home as the Ford Escape. But in fact this was not a home-built model at all, as it was jointly developed with the Japanese – this time Mazda, a manufacturer in which Ford owned a controlling share. The Escape was built in Japan and Mazda got its own version to sell, the Tribute. The result was a four-door crossover SUV that Ford pitched as an entry-level model below the Explorer. But the Escape was not one of the company's more successful lines being particularly handicapped by the lack of a diesel engine. Buyers were offered only petrol units in four-cylinder 2-litre (122ci) or V6 3-litre (183ci) form. US sales were adequate, in Europe they were minuscule.

Opposite page and left: Ford's answer to the Japanese 'soft-roaders' was the Escape, 2001 versions being seen here.

Below and bottom: GMC's Envoy, launched in 1999, was the luxury version of the Jimmy mid-sized SUV.

General Motors, meanwhile, saw a simple solution to the rise of the executive SUV – add extra specification to its existing model lines. As far as the full-size Chevrolet Tahoe/GMC Yukon was concerned, the first move was to produce a new range-topping model, the Denali, in 1998. GM then went upmarket by adding an SUV to one of its most admired luxury brands – Cadillac. Launched for 1999, the Cadillac Escalade was very similar to the Denali, though vertical rear doors added for the 2000 model year gave it some distinction.

The mid-size SUV line got the upmarket treatment too. At the same time as it unveiled the Cadillac Escalade, GM went to work on its Blazer/Jimmy line, producing the GMC Envoy. Taking the version fitted with the 4.3-litre (262ci) 190hp V6 as its base, the Envoy was swathed in luxury. Of course it got the two-tone leather interior, wood trim, auto-levelling suspension and the like that one could find in its rivals, but among the more interesting additions was a telematics system called OnStar. No matter what time of day or night, an Envoy driver could call OnStar on their cell phone and be given everything from journey directions to a suitable place to stop for dinner, with the table being booked in time for their arrival.

A year after the launch of the Envoy, Chevrolet produced its version of the luxury SUV. 1999 saw the debut of the TrailBlazer, basically the GMC Envoy but wearing the Chevy badge. It had its own distinct alloy wheels to go with the familiar upgrades, topped by a two-tone leather interior and with a particularly impressive sound system on the options list. Made by Bose, it was linked to a six-disc CD changer in the centre console and boasted audio controls on the steering wheel.

Above and below: The all-new 1999 Grand Cherokee featured a revolutionary four-wheel-drive system, the Quadra-Drive unit, that could direct all of the vehicle's power to a single wheel if conditions demanded.

While all this was going on, one American SUV builder appeared to be ignoring the rise of the executive line – a manufacturer that has featured heavily throughout our story. Chrysler Jeep stuck to doing what it knew best – producing vehicles that like Land Rover offered on-road performance combined with serious off-road capability. There was a new model however – the second generation Grand Cherokee hitting the market in 1999. A year

earlier at the model's US introduction Jeep had laid out its pitch in the clearest possible terms, showing journalists a video in which the new Grand Cherokee charged confidently through a muddy landscape while a rival became stuck fast – that rival being the rather more upmarket Mercedes ML. Whichever Chrysler official authorized the release of the film must have soon wished for the benefit of hindsight – months later Mercedes-Benz took over the entire Chrysler company and all trace of the video disappeared. The message was now that Grand Cherokee and ML were very different products competing in different markets.

Though it looked similar to its predecessor, the 1999 Grand Cherokee was indeed all-new. The 4-litre (244ci) base engine remained, but it was now joined by a new 4.7-litre (288ci) V8 unit, weighing significantly less than its predecessor but producing 15 more horses, up to 235hp, and taking less fuel to do so. As might be expected considering the Jeep's heritage, the solid axles remained to ensure proper off-road ability, but one aspect of the newcomer attracted much interest – its four-wheel-drive system. The Quadra-Drive unit could if necessary direct 100 per cent of the power available to a single wheel, if that was the only wheel offering any

grip. It was a permanently activated unit, though in normal use most of the power went to the rear wheels. The axles also boasted a new device, dubbed Vari-Lok and controlling the amount of power applied – previously the brakes had been used to retard the engine's output, so now the unit could carry on working even while the vehicle was under braking. One journalist dubbed the system 'a work of genius'.

Despite the Grand Cherokee's traditional design, Chrysler did not ignore the executive trend, but just embraced it in a different way. The management felt that Jeep was not the right badge for a road-biased upmarket SUV. The more sporting-orientated Dodge brand, which Chrysler also owned, was a much better fit. So in 1998 the Dodge Durango appeared in the market. It was created from the existing Dodge Dakota truck, and was immediately dubbed by those in the know as a serious Ford Explorer competitor. This was one big SUV, with seating for up to eight. Power was provided by a typically muscle-bound V8 engine of 5.9 litres (360ci) which pumped out 245 horses, good enough for a sub-nine second 0-60mph (97kph) time. Other more basic aspects certainly found favour with American reviewers, one waxing lyrical over the Durango's nine cupholders, 'one big enough to hold a movie-sized container of popcorn'.

The success of the Mercedes ML and BMW X5 had firmly established the premium SUV sector, and had quickly led to an explosion of new model derivatives as every existing manufacturer clamoured to climb aboard the upmarket 4x4 bandwagon. But the arrival in 2002 of a new name to the market showed just how far the SUV concept had changed. For this brand to build an SUV was even more revolutionary than Mercedes' arrival in the marketplace five years earlier. The manufacturer in question was the renowned German firm of Porsche. Even if you do not know much about cars, you will know the shape of the Porsche 911, a low, curvy mid-engined sporting coupé. Its basic profile has not changed since its launch four decades ago, yet even today it still boasts supercar status. You buy a Porsche as much for the history, the decades of Le Mans 24-hour racing success, the iconic status equal to Ferrari, as you do for the performance, yet you get the performance as well.

Above: Seeking to maintain Jeep's off-road identity, Chrysler used its Dodge brand to market an upmarket SUV, the Durango of 1998.

Left: The Durango was praised for its powerful V8 engine, its seating for up to eight, and its capacious cupholders!

Porsche traditionalists had not been over-impressed when the marque launched a 'more affordable' roadster, the Boxster, so when news of an SUV project leaked out, controversy erupted. To satisfy the doubters, this SUV had to be something special, and it certainly was. The Cayenne came in three versions, and even the standard model was powered by a 3.2-litre (195ci) V6 petrol engine with 246hp and a 9.1-second 0-60mph (97kph) time. The 4.5-litre (275ci) V8 petrol engine offered 335hp and sent the Cayenne through 60mph (97kph) from rest in 6.8 seconds. But topping them all was a turbo with no less than 443hp, slicing the 0-60mph (97kph) time to under six seconds and boasting a terminal speed of 165mph (266kph) – bordering on supercar territory. Now the critics changed tack, asking who would pay the £50,000 ($90,000) asking price for such an SUV? The answer has proven to be lots of people, especially as the base

model Cayennes in America start at not much more than £22,500 ($40,000), which for this badge is highly affordable. It can go off-road too, boasting a low-range gearbox.

Within two years of the Cayenne's launch the wealthy had adopted it as an accessory that was every bit as desirable as its sports car siblings. Today Porsche sells more Cayennes than any other model, including the 911, and if you visit any venue where the rich gather together, such as St Moritz, Switzerland in the ski season, many a Cayenne will be spotted.

The transformation was complete – in half a century the 4x4 had undergone a metamorphosis, evolving from a spartan, tough machine carrying plenty of passengers in a crude station-wagon body to executive heavyweights with supremely plush interiors and the ability to outrun sports cars. The age of the Sports-Utility Vehicle had truly arrived.

**2002 Porsche
Cayenne Turbo**
Engine:
V8 petrol
Capacity:
4511cc (275ci)
Power:
443hp
Transmission:
6-speed tiptronic,
permanent 4WD
Construction:
Unitary
Suspension:
Independent all round,
wishbones, coil springs
Brakes:
Discs all round
Weight:
5193lb (2355kg)
Top speed:
165mph (266kph)
0-62mph (100kph):
5.6 seconds

6 Today's SUV – Controversial but Everywhere

As an experiment, my son and I surveyed the number of SUVs spotted during a five-mile journey to his school through a reasonably urban landscape over the course of a week. The daily average was 54, a typical day's count producing nine Land Rover Discoveries, five Freelanders, seven Range Rovers, five Toyota RAV4s, a trio of Land Cruisers, nine Honda CR-Vs, a quartet of Jeep Grand Cherokees, along with a Volvo XC90, BMW X5, Mercedes ML, Nissan X-Trail, Mitsubishi Shogun...

Above and below: The latest SUV invasion has come from Korean manufacturers – these pictures show Hyundai's oddly named Terracan.

As these statistics indicate, at the start of the 21st century the SUV remains the one consistently growing segment in the motoring market. What makes this remarkable is that such growth comes in the face of growing protests against the SUV, generally led by environmentalists, and a campaign that on both sides of the Atlantic has become more co-ordinated and better organized. And with global warming and other environmental concerns now reaching the top of the political agenda, anti-SUV campaigners are enjoying the rich oxygen of publicity for their efforts.

In the USA such protests have been apparent for some years. If you enter the phrase 'anti-suv' into an internet search engine, it brings up page after page of sites dedicated to battling the 4x4 vehicle, perhaps one of the most notable being that of a group of Christians campaigning under the banner 'What Would Jesus Drive?' Such sites generally include lurid anti-SUV quotes such as 'If everyone in the U.S. who drives an SUV drove a car instead, we could cut out Middle Eastern oil imports entirely.'

Safety is another area in which the SUV is challenged, and protestors were given extra ammunition in 2003 when the head of America's National Highway Traffic Safety Administration, Jeffrey W. Runge, sharply criticized the safety of SUVs in an interview with the *Wall Street Journal*. He said that the vehicles' high centre of gravity made them three times as likely to roll over as cars. But ignoring the arguments of the environmentalists, Runge instead used his speech to call for more regulation of the safety features of SUVs, something that US manufacturers had previously managed to avoid – taking full benefit of the different official classification of 'trucks' and cars.

A study by the NHTSA into the effects of SUVs colliding with other vehicles in an accident added to the pressure, concluding that 2000 people killed in such crashes would have survived if their vehicles had been hit by a heavy car instead of a heavy SUV – the equivalent of five per cent of annual traffic fatalities. The signs were that the motor industry was listening; when Ford launched its enormous Excursion in 2003, its front and rear were specifically

designed to stop smaller vehicles from sliding under it in an accident.

Meanwhile the anti-SUV argument had gained ground in Europe, particularly in Britain. A simmering antipathy between environmentalists, safety campaigners and SUV owners erupted into action in 2004 with a series of protests targeting what the anti-SUV faction dubbed 'Chelsea Tractors', the name alluding to a particularly affluent district of London in which many residents owned SUVs. Most of the protests have been good-natured, for example following the US example of handing out spoof parking tickets citing 'poor vehicle choice', while one group even spent a morning at the kerb side offering to spray 'free mud' onto SUVs to make the vehicles look more in touch with their off-road capabilities. But Land Rover has also suffered picketing of its dealers and even an occupation of its vehicle production line by Greenpeace activists.

Reaction from the industry to such protests was initially slow, but as this book went to press the response was gaining ground. The manufacturer fight-back has focused on what they dub ill-informed criticism of SUVs, particularly a 'one-size-fits-all attitude' demonstrated by protestors. Honda was one of the first to go on the offensive, arguing that its CR-V took up less road space than many family cars, had earned better scores than many cars for both occupant safety and pedestrian safety in European industry crash tests, and also boasted lower CO_2 emissions. Toyota put a similar view in a specially produced DVD entitled 'Face The Facts About 4x4s'.

Yet while this debate has raged, SUV sales, particularly in Europe, have continued to climb, encouraging more and more entries to the SUV market. One possible reason was identified by the management of Korean manufacturer Kia at the UK launch of their new Sportage in 2005. 'Basically, people don't like to be told what they can and can't buy,' they stated.

Kia is a leading representative of the latest significant newcomer to the SUV market, South Korea. Both Kia and its now parent company,

Hyundai, have in the past few years secured a significant slice of the European market, while its presence is steadily growing in the United States.

Hyundai's early history was one of assembling cars and trucks in its home country for Ford, and later manufacturing old-model Mitsubishis under its own badge. Hyundai first started exporting cars to America in 1986, but the early SUV, the Galloper (a rebadged Mitsubishi Shogun), generally stayed in markets closer to home. It did sell reasonably well in Europe until its replacement was unveiled in 1999 at the Seoul Motor Show, and given the somewhat odd name of Terracan. Available in Europe since 2001, but not in the USA (some have suggested that a name that appears to combine the phrases 'terror' and 'tin-can' would not be the best guarantee of sales success!), the Terracan is effectively an evolution of the Galloper and still sits on its old-style ladder frame. Power is supplied by either a 3497cc (213ci) V6 petrol engine of 195hp or a 2902cc (177ci) diesel of 150hp (though UK buyers are not offered the petrol unit), driving a selectable four-wheel-drive system.

Hyundai's American SUV sales rely on two models, the Santa Fe originally unveiled at the 2000 Detroit Motor Show and the rather more recent Tucson, revealed in 2004 as a compact 'crossover' style machine. The Santa Fe is typical of the modern breed of SUVs with on-road performance and refinement assuming prominence. So while there is plenty of room inside it and trim and equipment levels are designed to attract, there is rather less for those who like to go off the beaten track, no low-range transfer gearbox, for example, or lockable differential. With engine choices stretching to 2.4 or 2.7-litre (146 or 165ci) petrol or 2.0-litre (122ci) diesel units, the Santa Fe looks tougher than it is, but for many buyers in today's market that is all that is required.

Top and above: Hyundai's Santa Fe offers plenty of comfort on the road but rather less off-road prowess.

Right: The Tucson is Hyundai's contender in the RAV4/CR-V market sector.

Below: A proper full-time four-wheel-drive system ensures that the Tucson is not 'all show and no go'.

The Tucson has found rather wider appeal – a compact SUV taking on the likes of Honda's CR-V and the Toyota RAV4, it has been praised for the fact that it does not just look like an off-roader, thanks to its electronically-controlled and lockable full-time four-wheel-drive. With a choice of 2.0 (121ci) and 2.7-litre (162ci) petrol engines or a 2-litre diesel, generous equipment and prices starting from £14,000 in the UK, $17,500 in the USA, the Tucson has found its niche in the market.

Kia has been making cars since the mid 1970s, and in the 1990s it produced a small 4x4 called the Rocsta. This was later upgraded to become the Retona, but remained little known outside its home market. More successful was the first SUV, a compact model called the Sportage, unveiled in 1991. Built on a ladder chassis and offered in both two- and four-door variants, it boasted selectable four-wheel-drive, a limited slip differential and diff locks, giving it competent performance off-road. But

while production spread to Europe, the Sportage could not rescue Kia's fortunes and by 1998 the company was virtually bankrupt.

Hyundai came to the rescue, taking control of its home rival and giving impetus to Kia's resurgence. Sportage production was ramped up again, and at the Chicago Motor Show of 2002 a big sister SUV was unveiled. The Sorento is closely related to Hyundai's Santa Fe. Still riding on a ladder frame it comes with automatically shifting four-wheel-drive that gives it serious off-road ability, as the author can testify having attended the launch event in a quarry in Scotland.

The Sorento is sold in America with a 3.5-litre (214ci) V6 petrol engine while European buyers are also offered a 2.5-litre (153ci) diesel. While not as refined on-road as some rivals, the Sorento's ability and its bargain basement price has seen the model contributing greatly to Kia's rapidly increasing fortunes, with the factory struggling to keep up with demand.

Most recently the Sorento has been joined by an all-new Sportage, launched in 2005. This is a very different beast from its predecessor, and a distant relation of a Hyundai, in this case the Terracan. The new Sportage also boasts competent off-road ability, including a lockable electronic four-wheel-drive system, despite abandoning the ladder-frame chassis design for a more road-friendly unibody

style. US buyers have a choice or 2.0 or 2.7-litre (146 or 165ci) petrol engines, Europeans can also choose a 2.0 diesel. US buyers have been impressed, the Sportage earning a 'best small SUV' award from industry analysts JD Power.

Other Korean manufacturers, such as Ssangyong, are also seeking their slices of the market, putting further pressure on the big US manufacturers as the influence of the Japanese has not diminished in the slightest. The year 2001 saw

an all-new version of the big-selling compact SUV, the Toyota RAV4. Standard power was a 2-litre (121ci) 147hp engine (though again European buyers were soon offered a 2.0 114hp diesel) and permanent four-wheel-drive remained in the mix, Toyota's engineers producing a powertrain capable of impressive performance both on- and off-road. Again style was the governing factor behind the RAV4's design, the two- and four-door versions being distinctly different-looking vehicles. They impressed the critics – America's *Consumer Reports* magazine, not exactly the greatest advocate of the SUV in the past, named the RAV4 as 'the best pick' in the US market, and the model has continued to sell in massive numbers across the globe. That success was expected to continue with the third generation, arriving in showrooms in early 2006.

Above: An idiosyncrasy of some SUVs, such as this Toyota RAV4, is the side-opening tailgate which is not always the most convenient arrangement.

Right: The 2004 version of Toyota's RAV4 pictured here made way for an all-new model at the end of 2005.

Left: Toyota distinguished its bigger Land Cruiser by adding the Amazon title to its name, and launched a new version in 2002.

Cruising the Amazon

Toyota's full-size 4x4 line, the Land Cruiser, has also progressed. The 90 Series, by now known as the Colorado, was replaced in 2002 by effectively a second-generation version. Toyota highlighted its improved on-road ability, but also the fact that the separate frame ensured that its ability to tackle more extreme conditions was not compromised – among the new electronic features was a device to help starting on steep hills. The engines included a new 4-litre (244ci) petrol unit that dropped the 0-60mph (97kph) acceleration time under 10 seconds while for the American market only there was a Lexus version, that today is offered alongside the RX 300 as the GS 470.

The bigger Land Cruiser 100 Series, now known as the Amazon, gained a new version in 2002 targeting the Range Rover and BMW X5. Power is supplied by a 4.7-litre (287ci) petrol engine offering 234hp, or a 4.2-litre (256ci) turbodiesel with 201hp, both driving through a four-speed automatic gearbox. The permanent four-wheel-drive includes manually-selectable high or low ratio transfer gears and lockable centre and rear differentials ensuring that despite its high levels of refinement, this Land Cruiser remains a truly capable off-roader. Curiously this version is not available in America, though US buyers can choose a different mid-sized Toyota SUV called the Highlander, first offered in 2001 and aimed directly at those moving up from a traditional passenger car. Effectively a more road-friendly version of the established 4Runner, it is bigger than its sister vehicle and is built on the same platform as the Lexus RX 300.

Below: Toyota's 90 Series Land Cruiser was replaced in 2002 by a second generation model, again offered in two- or four-door varieties.

Left: The Land Cruiser Amazon, this a 2003 model, targets such competitors as Range Rover and BMW's X5.

Above: Not offered in Europe, but selling strongly in the USA, is the Lexus GX 470, which was effectively a smaller sister to the LX 470 and was created to suit the demands of American drivers.

The late arrival into the SUV market of Toyota's big rival Honda was easily offset by the success of the CR-V, so much so that in 1998 it gained a sister. The HR-V is a bit of an odd one out – aimed squarely at the recreational end of the market, it is a compact model, and while it has a proper four-wheel-drive system, its low-slung profile means that it is not greatly practical if you want to traverse much more than a muddy field. Even Honda appeared unsure about its creation – when the four-door version launched a year after the two-door, the official press-pack stated that it had lost none of the 'love-it-or-loathe-it, difficult-to-categorize styling'. Today detractors still dub the HR-V as more car than SUV, and rumours suggest the model line is not long for the market.

The CR-V, however, has flourished. A second generation model arrived in 2002, built in Britain and easily distinguishable from its predecessor by the more aerodynamic body. It was constructed on a platform shared with the Civic family hatch, which improved its handling, while the 2.0-litre (122ci) petrol engine saw its power increased to 149hp yet with lower emissions levels. But European customers had to wait until 2005 for a diesel option, a 2.2-litre (134ci) 139hp unit. Meanwhile in America

buyers got a new Honda model from 2002, the Pilot, but this 3471cc (212ci) V6-engined four-door with its full-time four-wheel-drive was not quite what it seemed – it had already been on sale for more than a year wearing Honda's upmarket Acura badge, and known as the MDX.

Right: Honda launched a new version of its best-selling CR-V in 2005, the biggest change being the availability of a diesel engine.

Much progress in the SUV market has been made by Mitsubishi. The original Shogun has progressed to a third-generation model and has proved a significant player in the growing popularity of SUVs as a whole. Today's version is offered as a two-door and a longer-wheelbase four-door, the latter boasting a foldaway third row of seats, while features such as the unibody construction, electronic four-wheel-drive, high-low transfer gearbox and locking centre differential ensure that it is equally assured on freeway or byway. Trim levels impress too, stretching up to the heavily loaded Warrior, designed to steal sales from more obvious luxury SUVs.

Style by Pinin

The success of the Shogun persuaded Mitsubishi management to expand the line, initially with the Shogun Pinin. The name is short for Pininfarina, the renowned Italian stylist most famous for creating the look of Ferrari. For Mitsubishi the company produced a compact SUV with a serious fashion factor, again its prime intention was to take on the likes of Land Rover's Freelander and the Honda CR-V. Supplied in either two- or four-door form and built at

Pininfarina's Italian factory, today's Pinin can be purchased with either full-time or a selectable four-wheel-drive transmission.

The success of the Shogun spawned a third line with North American buyers most in its sights. The Shogun Sport, sold in the US as the Montero Sport, sits neatly in the line-up between Pinin and full-sized Shogun, and – as its name suggests – is aimed squarely at the leisure set. It seats five, and with its lower-line roof was long seen as a kind of large estate car with four-wheel-drive ability. Yet it has since been joined by a new SUV targeted mainly to satisfy those who want SUV looks but not necessarily the versatility. The Outlander retains four-wheel-drive, but its much lower shell, with less ground clearance, and bold front-end styling gives this vehicle a very distinctive presence on the road.

Above: Ancient buildings seem to appeal to photographers of SUVs! This is an official press shot of Mitsubishi's Shogun.

2005 Mitsubishi Shogun Pinin 1.8 MPI

Engine:
in-line 4-cyl petrol
Capacity:
1834cc (112ci)
Power:
113hp
Transmission:
5-speed manual,
permanent 4WD
Construction:
Semi-unitary
Suspension:
Front wishbones, coil springs, rear solid axle, coil springs
Brakes:
Front disc, rear drum
Weight:
2822lb (1280kg)
Top speed:
96mph (154kph)
0-62mph (100kph):
11.9 seconds

Left: The Pinin is compact and stylish, thanks to the skilled pen of Italian master Sergio Pininfarina.

Top, above and above right: Suzuki widened its SUV range in 1997 with a larger model, unsurprisingly dubbed the Grand Vitara.

Other Japanese manufacturers have generally maintained their presence in the market by enhancing existing products. Suzuki's long-selling Vitara was joined by a bigger sister, the Grand Vitara, in 1997. This was a four-door and effectively a logical development of the smaller model. Before long it spawned many variants, not least a seven-

seater first shown on the 2000 motor show circuit and since sold as the XL-7. As this book goes to press the third generation of the Grand Vitara is debuting in Europe, and it is very different from its predecessors. While still offered in two- and four-door forms, the separate chassis has gone. Its replacement is a unitary shell both longer and wider

than the outgoing model's but with a ladder frame built into it to maintain off-road ability. The two- or four-wheel-drive options have made way for a permanent four-wheel-drive unit, though the two-door, pitched as a 'soft-roader' for primarily tarmac use, does without a central differential lock.

A smaller Suzuki remains on the European market, but it's no longer the Vitara. In its place has come the Jimny, reviving one of Suzuki's oldest model names and applied to one of the smallest SUVs on the market. A definite recreational vehicle, the Jimny can be bought in two- or four-door body styles and as a softback. Just one engine option is available, a 1.3-litre (79ci) petrol unit.

After its run-ins with consumer groups through the late 1990s Isuzu has also stabilized its position on the US market, making the most of its tie-up with General Motors. In Europe the brand is best known for its pick-up trucks, though the Trooper SUV did provide the basis for GM's first European SUV, sold until 2003 as the Vauxhall/Opel Frontera. Americans have proven to be big fans of Isuzu's Ascender. It is sold as a five- or seven-seater and powered as standard by an in-line six-cylinder engine of 275hp, though a 290hp V8 is also available. Both units are matched to permanent four-wheel-drive transmission.

Top and above: Suzuki's current small SUV has revived one of the marque's oldest model names, the Jimny.

Left: Just one engine variant is available in the Jimny, a 1.3-litre petrol unit.

Right: The latest Nissan Patrol launched in 2005. It was updated and restyled but remained a go-anywhere vehicle.

Above: The Nissan Terrano II is an effective 4x4 but less refined than some of its more recent sister models.

Right: Nissan's X-Trail combines true 4x4 practicality with SUV style and equipment, satellite navigation being a popular add-on.

The Japanese manufacturer to pursue the rationale of the SUV most assiduously, however, has been Nissan. In America four different models are currently offered, while Europeans choose from five model lines, remarkably still led by the tough Land Cruiser rival, the Patrol. The sixth-generation Patrol launched in 2004, and while the most well-appointed version yet, it remains the most utilitarian of today's Nissan SUVs. The Patrol is bought mainly for its abilities, typified by the 3-litre (153ci) diesel engine powering permanent four-wheel-drive. Also remaining in the range is the Patrol's smaller sister and the vehicle that spawned Ford's first Maverick compact SUV, the Terrano. Today's version is a two- or four-door vehicle with a choice of two diesel engines, but no petrol unit. It is short on refinement, but that is no problem as Nissan has since come up with new models to suit today's mainstream tastes.

The first was launched in 2001 as the X-Trail, a mid-sized vehicle and yet another contender for the title owned by Land Rover's Freelander. While stylish compared to its elder sisters, the X-Trail is also practical, boasting a three-mode four-wheel-drive system that goes from two-wheel format on the blacktop to locked all-wheel traction when the going gets really tough. It only comes in four-door form, and with 2.0 (122ci) and 2.5 (153ci) petrol engines or a 2.2-litre (134ci) diesel. Unless, that is, you buy one in Japan, where a turbocharged version is also offered pumping out 280hp.

Americans cannot buy the X-Trail at all, but they are offered its bigger and newer sister, the Pathfinder. Again this sits on the rugged side of the SUV line as a sort of halfway house between Terrano and Patrol. Its off-road ability outshines its blacktop performance, but it does seat seven occupants – though the third-row seats are really only big enough for children. In America the only propulsion option is a 4-litre (244ci) V6 of 270hp, but Europeans have the alternative of a 171hp 2.5 diesel.

There are a pair of Nissan SUVs available to US buyers but not to Europeans – the Armada and the Xterra. The Armada is quite simply massive, more than 17 feet (5182mm) in length and able to take eight occupants. It's powered by a 305hp 5.6-litre (342ci) V8 petrol engine, yet despite its gargantuan dimensions it can be purchased in two-wheel-drive format as well as the traditional 4WD. However, its low-slung shell does not aid its progress when the going gets rough. Its not-much-smaller sister the Xterra remains one of the few SUVs around today developed from a pick-up truck. It's again available in either two- or four-wheel drive format and propelled by a 4-litre (244ci) V6 of 265hp.

Above: One of Nissan's newest and most radical SUVs is the Murano, launched in 2004.

Below: The Murano shares styling cues, and its engine, with the much desired Nissan 350Z coupé sports car.

Then there is the Murano, launched globally in 2004 and quite unlike any SUV that Nissan has previously made. In fact its closest relation is the 350Z, a sports coupé, both using the same 3.5-litre (214ci) V6 petrol engine, of 245hp in the Murano. Many observers see echoes of the 350Z in the Murano's highly curvy shell, a look clearly intended to rival the Lexus RX 300. On the road it's a front-wheel-drive machine, but four-wheel-drive is always present when needed. On the American market the Murano is also sold as an Infiniti model, where it is known as the FX and sits alongside the QX56, which is effectively an upmarket Armada.

All this adds up to major competition for the American brands, but it is competition that seems to have created little reaction. Today's US SUVs are generally little more than newer and improved versions of the truck-inspired vehicles that have been around for some time – a reason being the different safety regulations for cars and 'light-trucks'. The Explorer, for example, has survived the Firestone tyres controversy and two updates to remain a central part of Ford's line-up today – no surprise as it has constantly topped the SUV sales chart in America. The 2002 revamp was significant as both the Explorer and its upmarket Mercury Mountaineer cousin were completely redesigned as a distinct model line, unlike their truck-derived predecessors. They boasted longer wheelbases, adding a third seat row.

In 2005 the Explorer was redesigned again on a new, stiffer and therefore more handling-friendly chassis, with distinctive exterior styling and a higher quality interior. It has gained a new powerplant too, a 4.6-litre (281ci) V8 with 292hp, some 53 up on its predecessor and put through a six-speed automatic gearbox. Yet it remains a traditionally-constructed SUV, and according to US automotive consultant George Peterson that is unlikely to change. 'What you'll find is that the body-on-frame vehicles like the Explorer, Expedition and Mercury Mountaineer are going to be the workhorses of the SUV category.

They are the vehicles that will be used to go off-roading or to tow heavy loads because the other vehicles are not quite as well positioned to be able to do that.'

The Escape remains in the range too, and has assumed the mantle of Ford's most prominent SUV, due in no small part to the launch in 2004 of a petrol-electric version, the first production SUV hybrid. The motor was based on technology developed by Toyota, which Ford obtained licences to use. Combining a 133hp petrol engine with the electric motor produces power close to the 200hp V6 of a standard Escape. Like Toyota's Prius car, the Escape hybrid has proved a huge success – sales in its first year were four times greater than Ford had budgeted for. Today the hybrid is sold alongside the regular Escape which can be bought in a 2.3-litre (140ci) four-cylinder engine form as well as the V6. An upmarket Mercury Mariner version is also sold.

Above: Ford saw sales of its Escape model rocket after a hybrid-engined version went on sale.

Left: Capacious and commodious, the Escape is a major player in the current Ford SUV range.

Larging it

The large Expedition continues today in virtually unchanged form, the last major redesign having been carried out in 2003 and adding such desirables as independent rear suspension. Detractors say that a Ford Expedition is what you drive if you want to dominate the road without buying a Hummer – the standard engine is a 5.4-litre (330ci) V8 of 300hp. Yet despite this claim an even bigger Ford SUV did exist until 2005. Launched in 2000 and called the Excursion, it was developed from the Super Duty pick-up truck and seated nine – at almost 19 feet (5790mm) long it outstretched even Chevrolet's Suburban. In the Excursion, the 5.4-litre (330ci) V8 was the entry-level motor – other variants included a 7.3-litre (445ci) V8 of 235hp, paradoxically a smaller 6.8-litre (415ci) V10 that offered 75 horses more than the 7.3, and, unusually for Ford, a 6-litre (366ci) diesel. The Excursion did not meet with unqualified success – many potential buyers discovered that it was too big to fit in their garages, and baulked at its 6680lb-plus (3020kg) weight. But the model survived until 2005, its demise prompting one US analyst to comment, 'I don't think anyone's going to go that big any more.'

Above: Ford's Expedition remains in the range as an SUV for those who want to dominate the road.

Below and below right: Could this be the end of an era? Many people believe Ford's enormous Excursion was the last of the truly big SUVs.

Ford's great rival General Motors has pursued a similar basic plan of evolution rather than revolution. GM's full-sized SUVs, the Chevrolet Tahoe and its GMC equivalent, the Yukon XL, remain in the line-up, as does their upmarket cousin, the Cadillac Escalade. Effectively they date back to 2000, when they were launched as second-generation models, again still using pick-up truck platforms as their base, but now powered by more compact units of 4.8 (293ci) and 5.3 litres (323ci). Today these produce 285 and 295hp respectively, while the two vehicles have attempted to keep pace with ever-strengthening opposition by regular trim upgrades and the addition of extra equipment. However, as this is written, all-new replacements are believed to be ready for launch, the new lineup including a hybrid variant of the Tahoe.

The Envoy and Trailblazer lines of 2002 continue too, and for a while they were joined by a third badge-engineered version, the Oldsmobile Bravada. But that model disappeared when GM shut down Oldsmobile in 2004. Today's Envoy and Trailblazer are powered by a 4.2-litre (256ci) petrol engine of 290hp, though a 'displacement on demand' 5.3-litre (323ci) V8 was also offered in 2005 – rather like Jeep's Hemi it has the ability to shut down a bank of cylinders to improve fuel economy under less demanding conditions. Meanwhile GMC now offers a seven-seater SUV on a longer body that it has named the Envoy XL.

For many years GM also continued to sell its small Tracker SUV, effectively a rebadged Suzuki, but 2002 saw its replacement with a new model, the Chevrolet Equinox. Still built at the joint Suzuki-GM plant in Canada, this crossover-style rival to the RAV4/Freelander is also made separately under two more of GM's vast collection of badges, Saturn and Pontiac, as respectively the Vue and the Torrent. Each boasts its own distinctive styling and engine options and in fact the Vue was first to appear in 2002, causing much interest in the US market because it mated its 3.0-litre (183ci) six-cylinder engine to a five-speed automatic transmission, the first such auto in a small SUV. More recent additions have included the use of a 3.5 (214ci) V6 sourced from Japanese rival Honda.

Above: Chevrolet's Tahoe is now appearing a little dated – this is a 2002 model.

Below: The Equinox is Chevrolet's compact SUV and is designed to target the Japanese soft-roaders.

Above: BMW's second-generation X5 of 2000 looked virtually the same as the original but major changes had taken place under the skin.

Below and below right: BMW's X5 interior upgrades were well received but the new transmission was much bigger news.

Across the Atlantic the Europeans have not rested on their laurels, particularly the premium manufacturers. BMW's X5 was updated in 2004. The external changes were subtle but underneath an entirely new four-wheel-drive system was added, dubbed xDrive. Unlike the previous system that split power 40-60 between the front and rear wheels, the new version offers continually variable drive, able to transfer 100 per cent to a single wheel if it is the only one offering grip. The engines were upgraded too, a new 4.4-litre (268ci) V8 325hp petrol sourced from the new 7 Series saloon, and soon joined by a 4.8-litre (293ci) of 355hp.

The xDrive unit was also employed in a new BMW SUV, the X3 launched in 2004 as a smaller sister to the X5 and yet another Freelander rival. Using much of the hardware of BMW's renowned 3 Series saloon, the X3 offers a wide choice of engines – 2.0 (122ci) 150hp, 2.5 (153ci) 190hp and 3.0 (183ci) 228hp petrol units and a 2.0 150hp diesel. But it has not been as universally well received as its larger stablemate, with criticism focusing on its ride quality and interior. More recent versions have sought to rectify these faults, while BMW is now gearing up for the launch of a new X5 possibly in late 2006.

BMW's great rival Mercedes waited until 2005 to update its ML. The all-new version is a major improvement on its predecessor, with a far superior on-road performance while losing none of its off-road capability. Engine choices comprise a 3.5-litre (214ci) 272hp V6 and a 5-litre (305ci) V8 with 306hp, with an entry-level 190hp diesel following close behind. The one possible drawback of the new version is in its seating – the seven seats offered in the original ML are no longer offered as even an option on the new variant.

Meanwhile two more European manufacturers have joined the rush for premium SUV sales. Swedish maker Volvo built its first SUV in 2002. With an eye on where most sales were expected to be generated, the XC90 was designed in the United States. This is a full-size vehicle able to carry seven, and it attracted immediate and fulsome praise for a driving experience very like a typical car, without sacrificing its ability to traverse rough and ready landscapes. With a range of effective petrol and diesel engines, and a general sense of quality and clever packaging evident throughout, the XC90 has been a major success for Volvo, with waiting lists stretching to many months.

Top: The second generation of the Mercedes ML launched in 2005 was worth waiting for, and was a major improvement on its predecessor.

Above: Modern Mercedes quality is evident in the cabin of the latest ML.

Left: Volvo got its market predictions just right before launching the XC90, an SUV that has enjoyed prodigious success from the outset.

Above: Volkswagen's Touareg has a very prestigious sister model – the Porsche Cayenne.

The other newcomer is Volkswagen, a belated entry to the market but arriving with a very effective machine in the Touareg. This full-size SUV is a close relation of Porsche's Cayenne (which itself has continued to confound the critics, producing 41 per cent of Porsche's entire sales in 2004). The doubters were equally unsure of VW's chances in the SUV market, but all have been forced to revise their views – the Touareg ticks all the boxes, scoring particularly on its build quality and its V10 diesel engine. This is offered as an alternative to the 3.2 (195ci) 236hp V6 and 4.2 (256ci) 305hp V8 petrol units, and the rare 6-litre (366ci) W12 of 440hp (UK buyers can also ask for an entry-level 2.0 [122ci] 172hp diesel). The larger diesel pushes out 308hp while its 550lbft of torque makes it able to pull very heavy loads, but its early history has not been all plain sailing – emissions issues forced Volkswagen to withdraw the motor temporarily from the US market in 2005.

What, finally of the two marques that dominated the early years of the SUV story? For Jeep, the current situation has effectively been more of the same, concentrating on its three model lines, the Wrangler for off-road fun enthusiasts, and the Cherokee and Grand Cherokee SUVs. Last completely redesigned in 2002 and gaining the Liberty name in the US, the Cherokee underwent a milder revamp in 2005, with new transmissions, a 2.8-litre (171ci) diesel replacing the previous 2.4-litre (146ci) version, and an upgraded interior. The new diesel is also used to power a sporty Cherokee variant the Renegade, that launched in 2005 with a restyled body.

Right: Jeep's Cherokee enjoyed its latest upgrade in 2005, notably adding a larger diesel engine and better transmissions.

Above: All the important
changes are under the shell
of the all-new 2005 version of
Jeep's Grand Cherokee.

Left: Jeep's new Commander
appears to represent a back-
to-basics approach to SUV
construction. Despite its more
utilitarian look, the Jeep
Commander makes use of all
the technology featured in its
Grand Cherokee sister.

Jeep in Command

As for the Grand Cherokee, Jeep's range-topping
line, 2005 marked the arrival of an all-new version. It
looks sportier than its predecessor, but the
significant changes are underneath. Like BMW's
xDrive, the latest Quadra-Drive II four-wheel-drive
system can transfer all available power to only one
wheel if required. A new independent front
suspension improves the Jeep's road manners, but
most tellingly the power options now include a 5.7-
litre (348ci) V-8 Hemi engine. While seemingly a gas
guzzler, this unit uses the Multi-Displacement
System (MDS), which can deactivate half the
cylinders during cruising and light acceleration to
increase fuel economy by up to 20 per cent. Other
power options include a Mercedes-sourced 3.0
(183ci) diesel. In one move, Chrysler has pitched its
dated lead model back into the limelight.

Meanwhile 2005 at last saw the launch of a new
Jeep, the Commander. Compared to its ever more
swept-back Cherokee sisters, the upright, square
look of the Commander initially appears to be a step
backwards, but it gives a clue to its capability.
Despite measuring up at less than two inches
(51mm) longer than the Grand Cherokee, the
Commander boasts seating for seven. A V6 and a
pair of V8 petrol engines provide the power, while
the transmission and suspension are taken from its
sister models, ensuring the newcomer boasts all the
off-road ability one expects from a Jeep.

Above: The addition of a V6 petrol engine got top billing when Land Rover updated the Freelander in 2001.

Below: Launched in 2004, the Land Rover Discovery III is a radically-styled replacement for its predecessor.

The Commander was expected to arrive in the UK in March 2006, to face a home-grown Land Rover range that has been through a major process of renewal. Of the five-way line-up offered to 2005 customers, only the Defender, Land Rover's workhorse, remains ostensibly the same as it was a decade earlier. The Freelander, which quickly became Land Rover's biggest-selling model following its launch, was heavily revised in 2001, both the two- and four-door variants gaining a V6 petrol engine, a new and better turbodiesel for markets outside America, and a new automatic transmission dubbed CommandShift. In 2004 a Sport version was added and its specification is not just skin-deep – the suspension is lower and stiffened, and it sits on new 18-inch wheels. But

bigger changes are on the horizon – late 2006 sees the launch of an all-new Freelander.

The Discovery has progressed through two generations. The Mk2 version of 1998 was only offered as a four-door. It measured up seven inches (178mm) longer and almost three (76mm) wider than its predecessor, but in terms of styling was only mildly updated. Underneath, however, there were major changes, benefiting from the electronic advances made with the Freelander to produce a better performance both off- and on-road – the latter was greatly aided by the fitting of air suspension.

The age of Discovery

The vehicle was certainly showing its age, however, and 2004 brought a radical solution in the Discovery III, known in the US as the LR3. A huge, slab-sided vehicle with love-it-or-hate it styling, the current Disco certainly has presence, but it is also a more practical machine than its predecessor. There is plenty of room for seven within – UK magazine *Auto Express* stated 'This is better at carrying people than a Renault Espace MPV,' while the two rear seats fold into the floor to create an enormous cargo area. And while this is the most road-tuned Discovery yet, it has lost none of its off-road prowess, the obvious aids, such as air suspension, being joined by new features including Terrain Response, a dial allowing the driver to select the vehicle's set-up depending on the landscape being traversed. UK motoring presenter Jeremy Clarkson proved just how effective the system was by driving a Discovery to the top of a mountain in Scotland for the BBC television programme *Top Gear*. On the road a 4.2-litre (256ci) V8 petrol engine of 295hp provides smooth and rapid progress but hauling along what is a very heavy vehicle (much of this, according to its designer Andy Wheel, due to modern safety requirements) produces an eye-opening fuel consumption figure of less than 18mpg (16lit/100km), so most buyers go for the 193hp 2.7-litre (165ci) diesel, which can stretch a gallon closer to 30 miles (48km). Americans can choose either a 4-litre (244ci) V6 of 216hp or a 300hp 4.4-litre (269ci) V8, but no diesel.

The Discovery III could now be considered an executive SUV knocking on the door of the Range Rover, but Land Rover's range-topper has also been upgraded. The third-generation Range Rover arrived in 2001, the major beneficiary of the short-lived ownership of Land Rover by the German manufacturer BMW. Some £300 million was invested in the creation of the new Range Rover but much of the technology of the newcomer also found its way to BMW's first SUV, the X5. The current Range Rover is nine inches (229mm) longer and almost two inches (51mm) higher than the previous version, but it also looks much sleeker, thanks to a new aerodynamic shell with all the sharp corners smoothed out. A five-inch (127mm) longer wheelbase adds extra interior space while occupants travel in comfort and with plenty of upmarket extras to keep them happy. Of course, as befits the Land Rover badge, the Range Rover still knocks rivals aside as a supreme off-roader, a prowess today assured by many gigabytes of electronics. Propelling the beast is a 4.4-litre (269ci) V8 of 305hp and a 400hp 4.2-litre (256ci) supercharged unit, both made by sister firm Jaguar, plus outside America a turbodiesel of 174hp – the remaining link with BMW as it is made by the German firm.

More recently the Range Rover has become a family, with the arrival in 2005 of the Range Rover Sport. A production successor to the Range Stormer concept car that toured the 2004 motor show circuit, and to the disappointment of many lacking the concept's supercar-style forward-hinging doors, the Sport is effectively everything you get from the Range Rover but in a slightly smaller, more athletic package. It offers the same engine options though the petrol units are slightly less powerful, with either 295 or 385hp. Conversely the diesel is rated at 188hp – not that this matters to US buyers. On the road the Sport is more assured than its bigger sister, off the beaten track it has equal ability. It's also cheaper – US Sport prices start at $57,000, compared to $75,000 for the Range Rover, while UK buyers can pay respectively £35,000 or £46,000 for the diesel variants.

So today's SUV buyer is seduced by a choice of models that has never been more varied. Yet while it seems that every manufacturer wants to build an SUV, the concerns over such vehicles remain, particularly their perceived environmental effects.

However, designers of tomorrow's generation of SUVs are alert to such concerns and are looking to exploit new technologies, such as hybrid propulsion systems, to keep the SUV centre stage. Despite world oil crises, a growing campaign of protests ever-louder against its very existence, and a host of other threats, the story of the SUV has by no means reached its conclusion. In fact, in all probability for the Sports-Utility Vehicle, this is only the end of the beginning...

Above: The third-generation Range Rover of today is closely related to the X5 manufactured by former company owner BMW. While its commercial rivals have multiplied, for many the Range Rover remains the ultimate upmarket SUV.

Below: The latest addition to the Range Rover range is the Sport, a slightly smaller, swifter version of its long-established sister.

Index